Praise

"Are you wondering how to enchant your audience? How to make a stronger impact in your next presentations? Phil's methodology is clear and priceless. Read this book and learn from probably the most enthusiastic and passionate business presentation specialist!"
   – **Catherine Marchand**, Executive VP, Merchandising & Design, Lacoste

"I used to waste days preparing business presentations, thinking there must be a better way. Thanks to Phil and his methods, I spend less time for better results. What a liberation!"
   – **Nicolas Beau**, Global Head, Watch and Fine Jewelry Business Development, CHANEL

"Many business-critical ideas are expressed poorly, hence they are hardly heard and change little. Phil Waknell's book is set to repair this injustice. If you need to lead through ideas, this book is for you."
   – **Isaac Getz**, Professor, ESCP Business School, and author of *Freedom, Inc.* and *Leadership Without Ego*

"The business world needs leaders, and leaders need this book. Phil Waknell will absolutely change the way you present. A surefire method for presentation success."
   – **Garr Reynolds**, author, *Presentation Zen*

"Edgar Morin said that the complex is something we cannot explain. When explained, the complex becomes evident. It is this process of transforming complexity into simplicity in communication that I've found in this book. And the only word to correctly describe this process is truly 'art'."
   – **Paulo Magalhães**, Founder and President, Common Home of Humanity

"When the Beatles sang about revolution and wanting to change the world, they might have had Phil Waknell's excellent new book, *Business Presentation Revolution*, in mind! Waknell, the Chief Inspiration Officer of presentation company Ideas on Stage, pulls back the curtain to reveal how you can capture hearts and minds, change the world – and, yes, even start a revolution by enhancing your public speaking skills using his powerful and revolutionary methods."

> – **Todd Cherches**, CEO of BigBlueGumball, and author of
> *VisuaLeadership: Leveraging the Power of Visual Thinking in Leadership and in Life*

"I've had the privilege of working with Phil for the past five years – his know-how and methodology are both essential and inspirational. Welcome to the revolution!"

> – **Christopher Bailey**, CEO, Colombus Consulting

"I wholeheartedly share the purpose of this book, to improve the way we do presentations. This book summarizes more than a decade of Phil's experience as a presentation coach, and the tools revealed in this book will make your presentations more effective and enjoyable – not only for you, but, most importantly, for your audience. As Founder of the WikiStage Conferences, if I could make all of our speakers read this book and prepare their talks based on it, I would do it. This is a revolution worth joining."

> – **Johannes Bittel**, Founder, WikiStage.org

"In business, we should all live and die by the words of Sir Michael Moritz of Sequoia Capital: 'If people can't tell stories, I don't think they succeed as leaders.' Fortunately for us, we have tools such as this book and people such as Phil Waknell to help us make sure the stories we have inside us can reach their audience and make an impact."

> – **Jean Bourcereau**, Managing Partner, Ventech

Business Presentation Revolution

The Bold New Way to Inspire Action, Online or on Stage

Phil Waknell

R^ethink

CONTENTS

INTRODUCTION

Welcome to the Revolution

Some people choose to spend their time spotting trains or collecting stamps, even if others believe there could be nothing more boring.

Since 2010, I have spent my time on business presentations: writing them, illustrating them, delivering them and helping thousands of others to do so. Like trainspotting and stamp-collecting, many people might assume this is boring because that's how they feel watching most presentations.

Unlike these optional pastimes, business presentations are a necessary part of daily life in most organizations. And because they are often boring and ineffective, presentations are an expensive problem, and a revolution is long overdue.

By picking up this book, you have taken the first step toward joining the Business Presentation Revolution and learning to feel as passionate about presentations as I do. My aims are to awaken the credible, creative speaker you can become, to share a simple yet powerful method to make your presentations stand out and succeed, and to give you the confidence to lead and to inspire your audiences to follow you.

 With the tools and techniques in this book, you can transform presentations from an unwelcome task into a pleasure, for you and your audiences, and thereby improve your results, motivate your teams and boost your career.

Learning by doing

You will not become a brilliant presenter just by reading this book from start to finish, just as you cannot learn to drive a car without ever getting into one. We learn better by doing than by reading or hearing. Throughout this book there are activities to perform, and I suggest that you take the time to perform them.

To further enrich your learning experience, there are many additional resources available on the accompanying website: **bpr-book.com**. These articles, videos, examples, templates and checklists will add to what you can read in this book, help you in your activities, and inspire you to keep working to become the best presenter you can be. I strongly encourage you to access these online resources as you read.

Leadership communication

Are you a leader? How can you tell?

It's simple: someone with no followers isn't a leader. You can't proclaim yourself a leader – those who choose to follow you, or not, define whether you are a leader.

 Leadership is the art of being followed.

This means making others want to follow you. Whereas managers can make people follow instructions, leaders get people to follow them – not because they have to, but because they want to.

You don't have to be a manager to be a leader. If you are selling products, services, ideas or yourself, you need to make your audience want to follow you and your ideas. A successful presenter, therefore, needs to be perceived as a leader worth following, and we all know we are unlikely to follow a speaker who is poorly prepared, who speaks unconvincingly, whose presentation is boring or whose slides hurt your eyes.

This book is for anyone who aspires to lead, who understands that strong communication skills are vital, and who realizes that the conventional wisdom has led most presentations to be boring and ineffective. It is for those who wish to stand out, to inspire and to make people want to follow them.

If that sounds like you, read on. The business world needs more people like you.

The presentation problem

Imagine you are watching your favorite movie. You are captivated by the combination of a brilliant story, fine acting and breathtaking images. At the end, you feel happy or fulfilled, and you remember a lot about the film even though it only told you a story.

Now imagine yourself in a meeting room, or a university, or a virtual meeting, listening to a presentation. How do you feel? Most likely, the only thing you remember afterwards is how bored you were and how much of your precious time you wasted.

Businesses, schools and organizations all around the world waste millions year after year because of bad presentations. If you add the time and money spent creating bad slides, delivering ineffective presentations, and attending meetings, conferences and lectures that waste your time, you will quickly realize that all around you, presentations are a problem.

Think of it in pure business terms. If meeting participants remember nothing and waste their time, and if conference participants sit there bored and praying for the coffee break or evening cocktail, the return on that investment is minimal.

If your sales pitch fails to make customers want to buy from you, your revenues will suffer. If your leadership presentation fails to inspire your employees, they won't be motivated to deliver on your strategy. And if your results presentation fails to convince analysts that your leadership, strategy and results are a good deal for shareholders, your stock price and company value could plummet. In all of these situations, you would not be succeeding as a leader, and that could affect your own career.

The impact of a good or bad presentation has never been greater, yet most presentations are a waste of everybody's time. We don't just have a problem – we have a huge problem.

After the revolution

Most business presentations have been poor for too long. I've helped business leaders around the world with their most important presentations for many years, and they have seen what a difference a powerful presentation can make. It is a real competitive advantage.

To give you a clear idea of how different a post-revolution presentation is, the Before and After the Revolution table outlines how applying the five key revolutions in this book will deliver results that are diametrically opposed to typical, boring business presentations.

The Business Presentation Revolution does require a little effort on your part, but it will be worth it. I can be so confident about this because on all continents, across many industries and functions, from healthcare to luxury, from sales to R&D, so many business presenters have already joined the revolution and seen the difference it makes to their success – and they refuse to turn back.

Once you've read this book, you will no longer wish to suffer through another boring pre-revolution presentation, or to inflict one on your audiences.

Before and After the Revolution

Before the Revolution	After the Revolution
Focused on information	Focused on transformation
All about the speaker and what they want	All about the audience and what they need
Long enough, based on what the speaker wants to say	Short enough, based on what the audience needs to hear
Aims to include everything the speaker wants to cover	Aims to keep the audience's attention throughout
As standardized as possible	As personalized as possible
A monologue	As interactive as possible
Create slides, then (perhaps) think about what to say	Choose what to say, then (perhaps) illustrate it with slides
Tell them a lot, but they remember a little	Tell them a little, and they remember a lot
Full of facts and figures	Only essential data, backed up with examples and anecdotes
Lots of text on the screen	Visual slides with a few words
What you project is what you share (via email or printout)	You project straightforward slides and share a clear document
Your audience sits through your presentation, trying hard to listen	Your audience listens attentively without even trying
Your audience can't wait for the presentation to be over	Your audience can't wait for your next presentation

The science of presenting

I'm not a motor mechanic. I don't play with my car's engine because I don't understand how it works in detail. I leave that to professionally trained experts. The human brain is far more complex than an engine, and we know far less about how it works. Trying to present without learning a little about how the brain works is like throwing a spanner into a car and hoping it will fix the brakes.

Don't worry, I'm not going to get all neurological here. I'm just going to give you a few highlights about what presenters need to know. I believe this is required knowledge for giving presentations because when you present, you're trying to change what's in your audience's brains in some way. The following points are my own conclusions based on reading many books and papers, as well as my own experience. If you need to see the science behind these simple statements, I recommend the excellent *Brain Rules* by John Medina and anything by Richard Mayer.

1. There is no such thing as "divided attention": there is "undivided attention," or distraction. If you don't have your audience's undivided attention, they won't properly understand or remember what you're saying.

2. Attention spans are short, even for interesting material, and almost zero for anything boring.

3. When it comes to presentations, two synonyms for "boring" are "typical" and "predictable".

4. Human beings cannot listen to one thing while reading another.[1]

5. We forget most of what we hear, very quickly.[2]

6. The more we say, the less people remember.[3]

Business presenters need to know what science knows about how audiences pay attention and how they learn. Most presenters don't work hard enough to gain or retain attention; they expect people to read and listen simultaneously, they don't use memorable images, their presentations are too long and they usually say too much for fear of leaving something out.

 A presentation is hard work. If the presenter doesn't put in the hard work, it will be hard work for the audience.

All of this can be doubly relevant for online presentations. Where a live audience might be able to pay attention to their boss for twenty minutes, that attention span may only be ten minutes in an online meeting, where the speaker doesn't know whether the participants are paying attention – and where the participants know the speaker doesn't know.

The tips in this book take into account how our brains work, focusing on making the audience fully attentive, and giving them the best chance of remembering you and your messages.

Empty your cup

Astute businesspeople will realize that a problem for some is an opportunity for others. If most presentations are mediocre at best, then a little effort can allow any presenter to shine.

Buying this book is an important first step. You've started to invest in yourself and your ability to lead others. You've probably seen and given many presentations before, so you likely have some preconceived ideas of what presentations should be as well as what doesn't work.

Before learning how to join the revolution and enjoy the competitive advantage of this new and better way of presenting, you first need to let go of the old approach. Make a conscious effort to throw away everything you thought you knew about presentations. Trash the old ideas of "one slide for three minutes," "seven bullets per slide" and "tell them what you're going to tell them, tell them, then tell them what you told them". If your cup is already full, you won't be able to pour anything new into it.

Five key revolutions

There are many things people need to change about the way we present, but I have distilled them into five major revolutions. If you make all these changes, you are set up for success. If you miss one, you risk failure.

It's not your presentation – it's theirs.
Each presentation should be personalized to its audience.
Make them the most important ingredient.

Aim not to inform, but to transform.
People forget most of what they hear almost immediately.
Focus on what you need them to believe, feel and do.

Prepare your storyline before your slides.
You're not there to comment on your slides.
Your slides exist to illustrate and reinforce what you say.

Don't confuse slides with documents.
Slides make poor documents, documents make poor slides, and a mix of both is doubly poor.

Aim not for perfect but for personal.
People prefer authenticity to perfection.
Be yourself: when you share, we care.

Each revolution underpins one of the five stages outlined in this book; together, they will serve as your guiding light as you follow the path to successful presentations.

Now it's time to discover the method that has already helped many aspiring leaders and saved many audiences from presentation pain, and which will revolutionize the way you present: the Presentation SCORE Method, or pSCORE for short.

pSCORE: The Presentation SCORE Method

Over several years, and many thousands of presentations for clients of all types, we've refined the presentation generation process we follow at Ideas on Stage into what we call the Presentation SCORE Method (or pSCORE) – a tried and tested way to create and deliver effective and memorable presentations. It's the method we use with our clients in many industries and functions, the method we teach them, and a method that has proved its worth time and time again.

We call it the Presentation SCORE Method because there are five key success criteria for a great presentation, and they make up the acronym SCORE: Simple, Clear, Original, Related and Enjoyable.

SIMPLE
The more you say, the less they remember,
so keep it short, simple and to the point.

CLEAR
Your objectives and key messages should be
obvious to everybody – including you.

ORIGINAL
Make your presentation stand out,
and people will remember it for longer.

RELATED
It's their presentation, not yours,
so make it relevant and useful for your audience.

ENJOYABLE
If the audience enjoys your talk,
they will pay more attention, and remember more.

If what you say, what you show and how you speak all meet these success criteria, your presentation will likely SCORE with your audience.

pSCORE is a method that will give you the best possible chance of achieving those goals.

Let's look at what success looks like for a business presentation, using the five pSCORE success criteria.

Simple

In recent years, TED talks have demonstrated that short presentations work better than long lectures, but this insight isn't new.

Take, for example, the Gettysburg Address by Abraham Lincoln – one of the most famous and well-respected speeches by any politician in history. How long was it? Just over two minutes.

Nobody ever complained that a business presentation was too short – the opposite is usually true, and the effectiveness of a presentation is usually inversely proportional to its length.

Talk isn't cheap. In business, time is money, and talk is expensive. Too many people spend too much of their time creating and sitting through long, ineffective presentations. That's not a wise investment, so keep your presentation as short as it can be to achieve your objectives. That's the first aspect of simplicity.

The second is to ensure that you don't say too much. The more you say, the less your audience will remember – and don't forget how good people are at forgetting what they hear during a presentation. If you're too ambitious and aim to convey information that's too complex, or too much of it, they may remember nothing because you emphasized nothing.

 Say little, but say it well and make it stick. Keep it simple in terms of time, objectives and messages, and you're well on the way to presentation success.

Clear

Keeping your objectives and messages simple and your presentation as short as it can be is a good start. In fact, just by having an objective you're already ahead of most presenters. However, there are still plenty of ways for these simple objectives and messages to get lost somewhere between the speaker and the audience.

▶ If the audience can't hear you, they won't understand your message.

▶ If you speak too quickly, they won't have time to think about what you're saying and what it means to them, and they'll forget each sentence as soon as the next begins.

▶ If you use complicated terms or concepts, or mispronounce words, they won't understand your message – or, worse, they might misunderstand it.

▶ If the text in your slides is too tiny for your audience to read, they will try, and fail, and think poorly of you – and while they are trying to decipher your unclear slides, they are not listening to you.

You should also have a clear structure so the audience is never lost in your presentation, wondering where you are and where you might be going. And, as part of that structure, make your key messages stand out to your audience. Don't expect them to guess what's most important – they may guess wrong, or they may not bother to guess at all.

 If the audience can hear and understand what you're telling and showing them, easily determine your key messages, and know where they are at all times in your presentation's structure, then you've achieved the goal of clarity. It sounds obvious, yet most presentations fail on at least one of these aspects.

Original

In the business world, many managers sit through multiple presentations every day. Most of those presentations are alike, meaning that none of them stands out and sticks in their memory.

Imagine you are making a proposal to a potential client. That client might have six vendors lined up to deliver their presentations, one after the other. If five of the presentations look and sound similar, but one of them stands out in some way, which are they likely to remember the next day?

For the audience, an original presentation makes a refreshing change from all the usual, boring ones. For you, the presenter, that same originality gives you a better chance of being remembered, and it gives your key messages a better chance of being considered and actioned.

Your presentation should stand out –
otherwise, it will fade away.

Related

When you spend time choosing and wrapping a gift for someone, it's not your gift – it's theirs. When you spend time writing a letter to someone, it's not your letter – it's theirs. Likewise, when you spend time preparing a presentation for an audience, it's not your presentation – it's theirs.

Your audience is the first magical ingredient in a successful presentation. This means that it should be tailored to them and their needs, it should meet their expectations wherever possible, and you should deliver it in a way that suits them and creates a connection between them and you. It should also be related to other items on the agenda, if appropriate, as well as the context in which you are presenting.

Know your audience, and prepare a presentation
specifically for them. When you care about their
experience and offer them a personalized gift, they
will receive it gratefully and care about it – and you.

Enjoyable

This might sound more relevant to a TED conference than to a serious business presentation, but "serious" does not have to be the opposite of "enjoyable." In fact, business can learn from theater, film, and modern conferences like TED and WikiStage: people pay more attention when they are enjoying themselves.

Think back to when I compared watching a movie to sitting through a presentation. The more enjoyable the movie seems to you, the more attention you pay to it, the less distracted you get and the more you remember.

The same is true for a presentation, or a speech, or a lecture, or a training course. The more the participants enjoy it, the more they will pay attention, and the more they will remember.

If you want your audience to take action, you first need their attention. And if you want their attention, make your presentation enjoyable to attend. Enjoyment leads to attention; attention leads to action.

That does not mean that you need to crack jokes or show them video clips from *Saturday Night Live*. Humor may have its place in some presentations, but not in all. An enjoyable presentation is one where the audience pays attention effortlessly.

When it comes to presenting, the opposite of "enjoyable" is "boring" and therefore "unsuccessful." In Section 3, we'll see how to make a presentation enjoyable without making it any less serious or business focused.

You might think that making your presentation Simple, Clear, Original and Related is enough, and making it Enjoyable is just the icing on the cake. I disagree: enjoyment is the key to the cake tin.

 If your presentation isn't enjoyable, it doesn't matter what you say because your audience won't be paying deep attention, and you'll be wasting your breath.

Five stages to presentation success

We will come back to the five pSCORE success criteria throughout the book, and you will see why we need to focus on them so strongly. For now, let's take a first look at pSCORE and start thinking about how we build a presentation that will SCORE with our audiences.

Business Presentation Revolution is organized around the five stages of pSCORE, each of which corresponds to one of the five key revolutions:

Section 1: Foundation covers the first steps of preparing a presentation, remembering that it's not yours – it's theirs. We'll therefore start by focusing on the audience, their needs and the context in which you'll be giving this presentation, and then setting transformational objectives. The foundation on which you should build the presentation is the key stage that most presenters skip in their haste to start typing their slides.

Section 2: Ideation builds on your foundation by generating ideas for what to say, show and do during your presentation to achieve your objectives, aiming not to inform but to transform your audience.

Section 3: Creation takes your ideas and shapes them into a compelling and effective storyline for your presentation, with storytelling techniques to gain and keep your audience's attention and to make your key messages memorable. By the end of this stage, you'll know what to say and in what order – and then you'll be able to consider whether your audience might benefit from some slides. Always create your story before your slides.

Section 4: Illustration takes your storyline and illustrates it powerfully, avoiding a confusing blend of slides and documents, and instead using effective slides and other visual aids where appropriate to make your messages more interesting and memorable. By the end of this stage, you'll have a finished presentation, knowing what to say and what to show.

Section 5: Connection helps you to prepare and rehearse ahead of your presentation, and to deliver it professionally and convincingly yet naturally. Your performance in front of your audience is just as important as what you say and what you show, and your connection with your audience is more important still.

Each section includes several chapters, and at the end of many of the chapters you'll find activities. Since humans learn more by doing than by reading, I recommend you take the time to go through these activities.

I suggest reading through the book from start to finish, and then going through it again as you prepare your next presentation, making sure you complete each chapter before moving on to the next one. While it's up to you how you read and use the book (it's not my book – it's yours), I have two humble requests:

1. Please don't skip the Foundation stage (Section 1). If you forget to prepare, prepare to be forgotten.

2. Please use the many supporting materials at **bpr-book.com**. In particular, before starting the first stage, I recommend you fill in the free Impactful Presenter Scorecard. It only takes a couple of minutes, and it will give you an idea of your current presentation skills.

Now it's time to get started. Think of a presentation you need to prepare soon, empty your mind of everything you might already have thought to say, and let's go through pSCORE, beginning with stage 1: Foundation.

1 FOUNDATION

It's not your presentation –
it's theirs.

1.1
START WITH ABC

The aim of the Foundation stage is to create a platform for success. If you build a house on sand, it will not be stable; likewise, if you start to prepare a presentation without understanding its context or its audience, you will be setting yourself up for failure. Even if you only spend a few minutes on your foundation, those will be the most important minutes you spend on your presentation.

By the end of this section, you'll have a clear transformational objective for your presentation and a good understanding of your audience, and you'll be ready to begin thinking about what to say.

The first step to reaching that point, though, is to forget about what you want to say. Put that to one side for now and focus on your audience, their burning needs and the context in which your presentation will happen – the ABC of presentation preparation:

- ▶ **Audience:** a clear and detailed understanding of the people who will watch and listen to your presentation.

- ▶ **Burning needs:** knowing what keeps these people awake at night, their problems and their objectives.

- ▶ **Context:** your context, the audience's context and the context of the presentation itself.

By focusing on your audience right from the start, instead of on yourself, you are laying the foundation for a successful presentation. As much as possible, try not to think of your audience's needs through the prism of your own situation. You'll have plenty of time to think about your own objectives and messages later in the process.

Let's look at what we need to know in each of these three areas.

Audience

Since it is your audience's presentation, not yours, you should understand whom you will be meeting, or to whom you will be presenting. If you prepare a presentation for your business customer, but their finance director unexpectedly joins the meeting too, your presentation likely won't satisfy them both. If you just deliver your standard pitch, they will know that you didn't take the time to tailor it to them.

I once received a call from a senior director at a food manufacturer asking Ideas on Stage to help him create a presentation for an external event. Knowing the company has several different communities (the media, nutritionists, distributors, etc.), each requiring different messaging, I asked who would be in the audience. He didn't know – and immediately realized that neither I nor he could begin to prepare a presentation without knowing who would be listening to it.

Here's another story. Marie, a specialist in leadership, was asked to give a presentation in Warsaw for a business association. She prepared almost everything well. Almost.

She had flown in the day before, checked through her storyline and her slides that evening, got a good night's sleep, and even remembered to bring an umbrella, which was useful because it was pouring rain as her taxi drew up at the hotel where she was due to present. (It doesn't look good to present with wet hair and clothes.)

Marie had arrived a good thirty minutes before her presentation was due to start so she could check the room, get comfortable, test the microphone and connect her PC to the projector. So far, so good.

Except that there was no projector.

As the audience hadn't arrived yet, Marie asked the hotel facilities manager where the projector was. Imagine Marie's face as the lady laughed and replied: "But why do you want to project anything? Your audience can't see!" Indeed, Marie hadn't researched her audience: without knowing it, she was about to present to an association for blind professionals.

Poor Marie had done everything except her ABC. In particular, she hadn't understood her audience. Remember her story next time you are tempted to skip this vital step.

Knowing who is in your audience is the first and most fundamental step in preparing your presentation. Only once you know them can you tailor your presentation and make it a personalized gift for them. It needs to be adapted to their tastes, their preferences and their situation.

When I visit companies to speak about presenting, I don't give the same talk to every company. I don't even give the same talk to every function in a company. They are all different, and while a standard talk would meet their needs, you should be more ambitious than just meeting their needs. You should aim to delight them.

A presentation is a gift. You could give everyone in your life a pair of socks for their birthday, but would that make them happy? Unlikely. Similarly, personalize your presentation for your specific audience and they will be delighted.

A standard presentation is equally irrelevant to every audience. If you don't care enough about them to personalize your talk, why should they care about you and what you are saying?

A last point on the audience: you should try to know more about each key person than just the name and title on their business card. How long have they been in their position? Are they looking for a promotion or trying to make a mark in a new role? Do they like golf, or tennis, or rugby? Do they speak any other languages? Believe it or not, all these elements have been useful in presentations I've worked on.

 The audience is the first magic ingredient of every presentation. It should address them specifically, and anything you say about yourself should only be there to show how you can resolve their problems and fulfill their needs or desires.

Burning needs

Before you can hope to interest your audience in whatever you are recommending, you must interest yourself in their problems, their burning needs.

▶ What keeps them awake at night?

▶ What do they urgently need to fix?

▶ What are their personal and professional objectives?

▶ What are their current challenges?

▶ What do they want from you or expect from your presentation? (This may be different than what you want from them, but don't think about yourself at this stage.)

▶ Perhaps they have a need they haven't identified yet.

If you are going to present to a Chief Financial Officer who has just announced bad quarterly results and is under pressure to deliver better numbers this quarter, you might have difficulty convincing them to support a project that requires immediate investment and only long-term benefits. If you don't know their challenges because you didn't research their burning needs well enough, you could be thrown out quickly, never to return. But if you understand their burning need, perhaps there is something you can present that will help solve their problem – or at least avoid making it worse.

Some years ago, I was called in by a cosmetics company that had a huge problem with its presentations. They thought the problem was slide design, and it's true that their slides were awful, but that wasn't the main reason for the presentation disaster that caused them to call me.

They had realized that one of their major customers, a large international chain, was ordering less and less from them, and store visits confirmed that they were focusing on competitor brands.

They assembled a team to consider how to get that customer to buy more from them, and they arranged a senior-level meeting with the customer to pitch these ideas.

The team came up with many fine suggestions, such as exclusive versions of their cosmetics that could only be bought in their stores, extra training for beauty consultants, promotions and special in-store materials… and they produced 253 slides (yes, 253) to show to the customer.

The slides, mostly copied and pasted from a spreadsheet, were among the worst I have ever seen (and I've seen many). But wait for the real problem.

They arrived in the meeting room, exchanged greetings, and then one team member began to connect his laptop to the projector.

The customer interjected: "If you don't mind, we would like to give our presentation first." The sales director naturally accepted, and the customer gave his presentation, which went like this:

I have two points to make.

Firstly, your terms and conditions in Italy are completely unacceptable. We will make no more orders on those terms.

Secondly, your logistics are terrible. When we place an order, we do not know when it will arrive, or even if it will arrive. If you want us to stock your products, please address these problems urgently.

That is all. Now please go ahead with your presentation.

The sales team looked nervously at each other. Nowhere in their 253 slides did they cover either of these topics.

The correct reaction would probably have been to thank them for sharing their concerns, ask for more details and examples, promise to look into them, and ask for another meeting perhaps two weeks later to cover in detail how they would address both points – and then to end the first meeting, without presenting.

What the team actually did was to go through all 253 of their entirely irrelevant slides, sharing ideas that did nothing to address the customer's burning needs. The fact that the slides were ugly, impossible to read and entirely forgettable was beside the point.

 If only they had done a little research into the customer's real burning needs, this presentation disaster might have been avoided.

Beyond what keeps them awake at night, your audience also has personal expectations from your presentation. If you fail to meet those expectations, you will be perceived to have failed, even if their objectives were not the same as yours. If you don't know their expectations, you are flying blind.

This is why it is often useful to have everyone outline their expectations and objectives at the beginning of a meeting or training course. Of course, knowing them beforehand is even better.

After you've finished your ABC, you'll outline your own objectives, and you'll see whether you are able to meet your objectives and your audience's. If you cannot meet their expectations, then at least say so at the beginning, explain why, and give them new and realistic expectations.

For now, just ensure you know your audience's burning needs, including their objectives for your presentation.

Context

If you misunderstand the context, you might as well not even turn up. This means the audience's business context, the personal context of each person in the room and your own context.

What's the context for a sales presentation? Has the client launched a Request For Proposal (RFP)? Are they speaking with other vendors? Do they already have a contract in place? How are their current supplier relationships? Are they at the start or end of their fiscal year? Are they looking to spend in this year to minimize tax liabilities or defer spending to next year so they can meet earnings goals? If you don't know the answers to these and other questions, you're not well prepared.

What are the individual contexts of the attendees? Does the buyer have targets to reduce the number of suppliers? Does the finance director have cost-savings targets? Does the negotiator need to sign a deal before leaving on vacation?

If you're pitching to an investor and hoping to raise capital for your start-up, what's the investor's context? Do they manage a fund that is at the beginning of its cycle or near the end? Have they just announced a new fund? Which other start-ups have they invested in? Do they have guidelines that state a minimum or maximum investment?

If you don't know your audience's context, you don't know your audience well enough, and you're not ready to present to them.

The second aspect of context is your own. Let's look at an example: you are the head of corporate responsibility for a major energy company, and your task is to have your company recognized as the most responsible one in the industry.

You put in place a program of green initiatives, safety measures, investment in renewable energy sources, etc. One year on, you have some encouraging results, and you decide to hold a major press conference to share them and get journalists to write about how responsible you are.

The audience: journalists. Their burning need: to write articles that their editors will publish and their readers will want to read. Their context: usually under time pressure and needing to find something newsworthy that will attract readers.

Just as the journalists are arriving at the airport ahead of your big press conference tomorrow, you hear the terrible news that one of your oil tankers has suffered a huge leak. Now, instead of being a responsible energy company, you are responsible for massive environmental destruction.

Your audience and their burning needs haven't changed. Do you give them the same positive "green" presentation you had carefully planned? Of course not. Your context has changed, and your presentation should reflect that new context.

That was an extreme example, but knowing your own context is always key. Are you desperate to raise capital or can you afford to wait? Are you near the end of your fiscal quarter and needing to close a sale before the end of the month? Are you addressing your employees as a well-known long-time CEO, or is this your first week in the company?

 If you don't take your own context into account, you are not in a position to set objectives for your presentation, and achieving the wrong objectives is no better than missing the right ones.

Lastly, the context also refers to the time and place of the meeting or presentation. If it is online, which meeting application will you need to use? If it is going be a live presentation, will it be in a small room or a large amphitheater – or a restaurant? Will there be a projector? A flipchart or whiteboard? A microphone? Loudspeakers? Is it early in the morning, when people are most receptive to new ideas, or early afternoon, when people are tired and need to be active to stay attentive? How long is your presentation expected to last? Is there time planned for questions and answers afterwards? Is anyone presenting before or after you? If so, what are they planning to cover?

 Making a success of any presentation or meeting starts with strong preparation. Get that right, and you'll have a strong foundation. To paraphrase an old saying: if you forget to prepare, prepare to be forgotten.

Activities: Start with ABC

Before you move on, and particularly if you are reading this for the second time and using it to prepare a presentation, the following activities will help you to get a clear understanding of your ABC.

You might find it useful to download the ABC template from the book website at **bpr-book.com** or draw it on a board or flipchart.

First, choose a presentation situation. This can be a presentation you need to prepare soon, one you have already given or a hypothetical situation. You might imagine that you need to present a recommendation to your company's Executive Board; for example, that you should buy a key competitor, or relocate to Lisbon, or invest in a new product line.

Next, answer the following questions. They may not all be relevant to your situation, and this is not an exhaustive list, but it is a good start.

Audience

1. Who are the key people in your audience?

2. Which company do they work for?

3. What are their job titles?

4. Who is the key decision-maker?

5. Who are your allies – and your opponents?

6. Check these people on LinkedIn and other websites to learn as much as you can about them, as human beings as well as professionals.

Burning needs

7. What is the state of their business? This can include their whole company and their specific function or division.

8. What keeps them awake at night? What are their major challenges and headaches?

9. How do their challenges, problems and concerns relate to you and your activities?

10. What do the key people expect from your presentation?

Context

11. Do the key people have relevant deadlines any time soon?

12. Is there anything else you should know about your audience's context – recent or planned product launches or projects, company performance, relevant announcements or news?

13. How well does your audience already know you and/or your company or department? Do you already have contracts or projects running?

14. At what time of day will you be speaking?

15. How long is your presentation expected to last? Is there time set aside for questions and answers?

16. Will your presentation be online, and, if so, which meeting solution will it use? If it is in-person, in what kind of room will your presentation take place?

17. Will anyone be speaking before and/or after you? If so, what will they be talking about?

18. Will you have a microphone? If so, what kind?

19. Will you have a projector or screen available? If so, is it best to use 16:9 or 4:3 slides?

20. Will you be able to use sound effects in videos or other media? (If so, you need to have loudspeakers available for an in-person presentation, or a suitable tested online meeting solution which supports the transmission of PC sound.)

As you answer these questions, you might find yourself asking and answering others. Some questions will be more relevant for some audiences than others, but by the end of the process you should know enough about your ABC to start setting your own objectives for your presentation – if a presentation is the right way to achieve them.

1.2
TRANSFORMATIONAL OBJECTIVES

Information versus transformation

What is your presentation's primary objective? Many presenters treat their talk as if it were a dental appointment: their sole aim is to get through it as quickly and painlessly as possible, escape mostly unharmed, then drink something cool or strong, or both.

Other presenters might say their aim is to share information: for example, to explain sales targets or business results.

It's important to dig a little deeper; when it comes to objectives, the most useful word is "why". Why are you explaining your sales targets? Is there something you want your audience to do differently? Perhaps just by knowing the targets they will behave differently or feel more motivated to achieve them. In which case, you've changed your audience – and maybe that change was your real objective.

Most presentations fail because they try to transmit information, which is more effectively achieved with a written document. We forget most of what we hear very quickly, and cannot rewind a live presenter, whereas when reading we can go at our own pace, re-read sentences if required, and take the necessary time not only to receive and understand the messages but also to reflect on them and their meaning for us.[4]

Oral presentations (with or without slides) are fantastic for inspiring, motivating and transforming audiences, but using an oral presentation to share information is like using a colander to carry water. While it is good for some things, this is not one of them. However, a presentation is an excellent way to change what people believe, feel and do. If you don't change your audience in any way, then you've wasted your time – and, worse still, you've wasted theirs.

Revolution #2, which we'll learn more about in Section 2, is: aim not to inform, but to transform. For example, if you're launching a new gadget that you hope will shake up your industry, your presentation's aim will not be to share information – number of pixels, processor speed, etc. – but to create desire and to make people buy your product and write articles recommending it. You'll want to generate feelings and actions. Your presentation will include information, but only the information you need to achieve those transformational objectives.

If your audience remembers all the gadget's specifications but does not want to buy it, would that count as a successful presentation? No. But, if they forget all the details yet still feel a strong desire to buy it, the answer becomes a resounding "Yes." It's therefore clear that the objective was not transmitting information but generating transformation.

When not to present

Fixing the presentation problem and joining the Business Presentation Revolution does not only mean creating and delivering better presentations. It also means knowing when to present – and when not to.

Far too many businesspeople still approach a presentation with the sole aim of sharing information. If you find yourself in that situation, ask yourself why your audience needs this information and what transformation you aim to achieve. If there is no transformation required but you still need to share information, then forget about an oral presentation: give them a written document and time to read it (and ideally a coffee too), and you'll find that more effective for everyone.

At Amazon, and many other companies who have followed their lead, meetings never include presentations.[5] Instead, meetings begin with a period of silence, during which participants read a six-page written document – with full paragraphs, not a set of slides – telling them all the background they need, the reason for the meeting and what they need to decide. (They read the document at the start of the meeting because Jeff Bezos realized that you can't rely on everybody to read the document thoroughly beforehand.)

After reading the document, everyone is literally on the same page, and they can then question its author, check their understanding, discuss the key points, reach agreement and leave before the coffee gets cold. Despite the added reading time at the start, these meetings are more effective. Nobody stands up to give a presentation because there's no point – and, therefore, no PowerPoint.

Never pollute a meeting with an unnecessary presentation, and never use a presentation to deliver information. Documents are for information-sharing, and meetings are for connections, discussions and decisions.

You do not always need a presentation, and when you do present, you don't always need slides. Use presentations only when they are the right way to achieve your objectives, never by default.

 Treat presentations not like a Swiss Army knife – mildly useful in many situations – but instead like a Samurai sword: highly effective but only in specific circumstances.

A simple way to set your objectives

If you've decided that a presentation is the right choice, and if you've done your ABC, it's time to set your objectives.

Complete this sentence:

"After this presentation, the audience will..."

Make sure the verb in the last part of the sentence is a "feeling" or "doing" verb. If you find yourself with the verb "know" (or something similar), ask yourself **why** they need to know this – and then complete the sentence again with the real objective.

- ▶ **Informational objective:** "After this presentation, my audience will know our corporate presentation style."

- ▶ **Transformational objective:** "After this presentation, my audience will successfully use our corporate presentation style every time."

Try to stick to one or two transformational objectives. If you chase too many rabbits, you probably won't catch any.

Objective flows

As you complete your presentation objective sentence with an action, you might realize that in order to take this action, your audience will need to feel something: urgency, fear, enthusiasm, confidence or desire, for example. You might therefore decide to complete the sentence a second time with a "feeling" verb.

This is not an additional, distinct objective, but part of what I call an "objective flow": the feeling leads to the action, and while the action is the desired end-result, provoking this feeling is necessary, not "nice to have."

When interviewing for a new position, your "action" objective could be:

"After this interview, the interviewer will offer me a job."

If the interviewer doesn't trust you, or isn't confident you can do the job, they won't choose to hire you; therefore, you might need to complement this "action" objective with a "feeling" objective that will lead them to hire you:

> "After this interview, the interviewer will trust me and feel confident and positive about my candidature."

To take the objective flow a step further, you might also need to provoke a belief that will generate these feelings which, in turn, will lead to the desired actions:

> "After this interview, the interviewer will believe I am an excellent candidate and will succeed in this position."

Remember that beliefs generate feelings, and feelings generate actions. We will develop this concept further in the Audience Transformation Roadmap in Section 2.

You'll notice how important it is to do your ABC first. Understanding the ABC allows you to choose the right objectives in terms of how you want to change your audience. You can't move them from where they are to where you want them to be without understanding where they are – that's the ABC. And if you don't understand where you want them to be, you'll never take them there – that's your objective(s). If you haven't got a clear objective, you certainly won't achieve it.

1.3
FOUNDATION: SUMMARY AND ACTIONS

The Foundation stage may not take long, but it is time too few presenters choose to spend. If you understand your audience, their burning needs and the context, and choose a few transformational objectives, then you are ready to start preparing your presentation. If not, you are shooting at an invisible target with both hands tied behind your back. Business productivity requires efficiency, but the Foundation stage is not a corner you can cut, it is the fastest path to success.

If you already understand that it's your audience's presentation, not yours, and you should personalize it for them based on who they are, their burning needs and the context, you are one step ahead of most presenters. If you also understand that presentations are not good ways to inform people, but powerful ways to transform them, you are ten steps ahead.

Before you get ahead of yourself, let's recap the key steps in the Foundation stage, and make sure you have clear transformational objectives for your presentation.

1. Revisit the ABC activities in Chapter 1.1, making sure you have a full understanding of your Audience, their Burning Needs, and the Context of the presentation.

2. Using this example presentation, complete this sentence:

   "After this presentation, the audience will..."

3. Check to see whether the verb is a "feeling" or "doing" word, as opposed to "know" or "be aware of".

   Good examples are "make," "do," "execute," "deliver," "sell," "perform," "succeed," "create," "feel," "believe" and "change."

4. Ask yourself the magic question: why? Why is it good for them to do what you stated in your completed sentence?

   If you realize that your sentence is a means to an end, but not the final objective, then start again from step 2.

5. If you have formulated a clear objective that stands up to the question "why," ask yourself whether it is your only key objective. If you need one more (or two more at the most), note down your first additional objective and start again from step 2 to create your second and perhaps third.

6. Try to establish an objective flow for each of your main objectives. Start from the action, then work backwards to define what they should feel and, finally, what they need to believe to feel that way and take those actions.

Now you have understood your ABC, and you have clear objectives on how you aim to transform your audience, you have a strong foundation on which you can build a successful presentation.

In the next section, we'll start to focus on what to say, show and do to achieve these objectives.

② IDEATION

Aim not to inform, but to **transform.**

2.1
THE CREATIVE PROCESS

The aim of the Ideation stage is to generate all the raw material you need so you are ready to begin creating your presentation. This means you need to find ideas – the raw material of a successful presentation.

The process outlined in this section will help you find many ideas, channel your thinking to ensure those ideas are relevant to your objectives, and even help you understand your true objectives more clearly.

By the end of this section, you'll know your objectives and your key messages, and you'll have plenty of ideas of what to say, show and do during your presentation to reach those objectives.

Switch off

In this chapter, we will discover the basis of the creative process and how to find better ideas to surprise and move our audience.

By this stage, we have one or more clear transformational objectives (or objective flows). What happens next is just as important.

What usually happens next is that the presenter opens PowerPoint and starts typing slide 1, hoping that by the time they reach the end they'll have something cohesive and effective. Unfortunately, hope is not a strategy. You shouldn't be creating slides until you know what you're going to say, but it's equally important to remember that many of us are more creative with a pen and some sticky notes or a flipchart than we are sitting at a screen. While there are all sorts of applications available to log your ideas, and some of them are helpful, none of them will help you to generate ideas.

 Switch off your screen, and switch on your creativity.

The four steps of creativity

If you are ready to be creative, then it's time to generate ideas for things to say, show and do to achieve your transformational objectives – and ways to make your presentation richer and more original. If you skip the Ideation stage, your presentation will end up flat, boring and unlikely to succeed.

Graham Wallas, co-founder of the London School of Economics, was one of the first people to assign a framework to the creative process. In his 1926 masterpiece *The Art of Thought*, the four steps he proposed were: preparation, incubation, illumination and verification.[6]

The process we use in pSCORE is slightly different and tailored to the presentation generation process. Hat tip to Ideas on Stage co-founder Pierre Morsa who first formalized these four steps, and opened my eyes to the importance of incubation.

Step 1: Research

Nobody can create a great presentation out of thin air. The best presenters combine outstanding presentation skills with vast knowledge and experience of their subjects and an ability to communicate them to their audiences. This is why we spent time researching our ABC, and in doing so we've already begun the Research step.

You might want to continue researching your audience, their company, their market and their competitors. You might also need to do more research about the subject of your presentation.

Step 2: Brainstorm

If research alone were sufficient, then all scientists and experts would craft great presentations. A visit to any medical congress will cure you of that belief.

The Brainstorm step will take the knowledge you collected in the Research step and transform it into creative presentation ideas. In the next chapter, you'll discover the Audience Transformation Roadmap, a fantastic tool to help you run a targeted brainstorm to imagine your presentation.

Step 3: Incubate

After the Brainstorm, you will have many ideas, but the creative process does not stop there. This step is paradoxical: without doing anything consciously, your subconscious brain will continue to work to assimilate all the information from the Research and Brainstorm steps. Who said doing nothing is a waste of time?

It's important to give your brain time to incubate your ideas, so try to do your Brainstorm a few days before you need to prepare your storyline.

Step 4: Output

This is the final step of the creative process, where you come back to your ideas and formulate them into a storyline. The ideas you have after the incubation period will often be better, stronger ideas than the ones you came up with during the initial brainstorm.

This Output step in the creativity process aligns with the Creation phase of pSCORE (Section 3 of this book) as you shape your ideas into a powerful storyline.

The list of activities for the Ideation stage comes at the end of this section. Before we get to that, it's time to introduce you to the Audience

Transformation Roadmap, a simple framework which has proven its worth time and again. The Roadmap may be the single most important part of this book, so it has a chapter all to itself. This is one you'll probably come back to again and again.

2.2
THE AUDIENCE TRANSFORMATION ROADMAP

Three magic ingredients

If there are three points that should appear in any presentation, those points are: the audience, the speaker and the transformation you aim to induce in your audience

In this chapter, we'll focus on how to transform your audience. Before we start brainstorming, it's important to think about the first two ingredients: the audience and the speaker. While you go through your creative process, keep asking yourself:

> "How can I build the audience and myself
> into this presentation?"

1. The audience

If your presentation could be given, word for word and slide for slide, to a different audience, then your audience isn't part of your presentation.

If you give a standard presentation, the audience will know it, and they won't feel special – worse, they will feel like you don't think they are special. And if they think you don't think they are special, they won't think *you're* special either. (You might need to read that last sentence again. I certainly did.)

While brainstorming, think of ways to get the audience involved: by asking them questions, by getting them to do something or by talking about them more than about yourself. This will help your audience to realize that it's not your presentation – it's theirs. And they will love you for it.

2. The speaker

If someone else could have given your presentation, word for word and slide for slide, then there is nothing of you in it. This is why, when writing speeches and creating presentations for leaders, I first get to know them, and when brainstorming with them, I make a particular effort to identify their own stories and feelings.

When giving training, I use many anecdotes, but they are all from my own experience. My colleagues deliver the same courses but use their own examples. It isn't personal if you're telling somebody else's story.

Even though it is your audience's presentation and you should make it about them as much as possible, when you are telling stories, make them your stories and invest yourself into your presentation. You are the second magic ingredient. Don't leave yourself out.

 As you use the Audience Transformation Roadmap, remember these first two magic ingredients and ask yourself how you can make this a presentation that only you can give and only to this audience.

Where is your audience?

As we've already seen in previous chapters, your aim is not to inform but to transform your audience somehow: from prospects into customers, from skeptics into believers, from observers into actors, or perhaps from unhappy employees into happy, motivated contributors.

Imagine your audience on one side of a river, the "before" side; your aim in your presentation or meeting is to take them to the other side, the "after" side.

You are not going to just stand on the "after" side and shout, "Hey, look at my great idea – come over here!" Unless your idea is truly fantastic, they're not going to swim across to find you. It's up to you to start from their side, provide the right stepping-stones to allow them to cross, and then guide them to your destination.

Too many presenters fail to transform their audiences because they start from their own level of expertise and knowledge, and their wisdom goes over their audience's heads. They are standing on their "after" bank of the river, shouting into the mist about how wonderful it is, and have no idea where the audience is or whether they can hear or understand them. That's no way to transform people.

 You can't take someone from point A to point B without starting from point A alongside them. And to do that, you need to know where point A is.

The good news is that you've already studied your ABC and you've done your research, so you know a lot about your audience and what's on their minds. You also have a good idea of your objective: how you want to transform them, or where you want to take them.

The next question is where your audience stands in relation to your objective. Let's say, for example, that you are the CEO of a 1,000-person company. Your audience is your employees; their burning need is to feel safe and secure; and the context is an exceptional all-employee online meeting during a particularly difficult quarter.

You've decided your objective for this presentation is:

"After this presentation, the audience will work harder to deliver more revenue and secure all our jobs."

You can now analyze where your audience is in relation to this objective before you deliver your presentation. Perhaps they are afraid or demotivated, or perhaps they don't even know how competitive the environment is.

Now let's say that, for the same presentation and with the same ABC, you decided on a different objective:

> "After this presentation, the audience will accept
> a voluntary pay cut of 10% to save the company."

Your audience will relate to this objective differently. In this case, you need to analyze their financial situation, how they feel about their salaries, what they know about the industry and the competition, and how much they trust you. This is why it is so important to go beyond your ABC and work out where your audience is in relation to where you want to take them.

Four steps to understanding

There are four simple yet powerful questions you can ask yourself to help you understand where your audience is before your presentation. In relation to your objectives, company, products, services, project, ideas, etc.:

1. What do they **know**?

   This relates to relevant facts that they know for certain before your presentation.

   For example, they may know the sales figures this quarter are 30% down versus last year.

2. What do they **believe**?

   This includes things they think they know but which we cannot put in the "know" section for one of the following reasons:
   - They are wrong.
   - They aren't sure.

- They are speculating about what might happen.
- They are making a judgment.

For example, still using the example of a CEO of a 1,000-person company:
- They believe you will take a bonus despite the poor results (wrong).
- They believe you've been looking for an excuse to reduce headcount (unsure).
- They believe you will announce job losses (speculation).
- They believe the company strategy is crazy (judgment).

3. What do they **feel**?

This is their emotional state as it relates to your presentation, before you begin.

For example, they may feel demotivated, afraid, angry, frustrated or pessimistic.

4. What do they **do**?

This relates to actions they take.

For example, they may focus on selling big long-term contracts that don't provide quick income, or they may accept long payment terms without negotiating, or they don't collaborate effectively to boost sales.

You can answer these questions using the Audience Transformation Roadmap, which you can draw on a board or flipchart. You can also fill it in on a computer or tablet (although remember that I recommend avoiding screens and computers while you're trying to be creative).

You can download an Audience Transformation Roadmap template from the *Business Presentation Revolution* website: **bpr-book.com.**

What they...	BEFORE	⟹	AFTER
...know			
...believe			
...feel			
...do			

The Audience Transformation Roadmap

After you have worked out what they know, believe, feel and do *before* your presentation, you will answer the same questions for your audience *after* your presentation. Remember that everything in your roadmap should relate to your objective(s) and the context. If you are presenting to request reimbursement approval for a new drug, it's probably irrelevant that the head of the advisory committee skis in the Alps every Christmas, but it may be relevant that they have a history of rejecting reimbursement requests for drugs seen as "me-too" products.

Using the Audience Transformation Roadmap

My Ideas on Stage colleagues and I have tested the structure of the Audience Transformation Roadmap over several years with a wide variety of customers and situations, and, despite its simplicity (or perhaps because of it), it is powerful when used well. Our experience shows, however, that there is definitely a best way to use it.

Always start at the top left, with what the audience knows beforehand, and work your way down to what they do before your presentation.

Imposing constraints on creativity makes us more creative, and this road-map is one such constraint, but sometimes ideas will come when you are not expecting them, and you should be prepared for this and not ignore them. If you find yourself identifying what your audience feels, for example, while you're working on what they believe, note it down in the "feel" box – otherwise you might forget that point – and then focus back on what they believe.

In the "know" and "believe" boxes, you might also think of things that they don't know or don't believe, and which are relevant to your presentation. Note them down too, either in a different color or with a big "X" next to them. They may come in handy later.

Once you have reached the bottom left and identified what they *do* before your presentation (and bear in mind that may be "nothing"), move to the bottom right and immediately identify what you want them to *do* after your presentation.

Then, move up a level and identify what they would need to *feel* in order to do those new or different things – or, if you are not requesting any particular action, just note what you need them to *feel* afterwards, which is often the positive opposite of what they felt before (pessimistic to optimistic, bored to enthusiastic, etc.).

Next, what do you want them to *believe* afterwards? Do they need to *believe* something different in order to *feel* and/or *do* what you wish? Or can they *feel* and *do* those things without changing what they *believed* before?

Finally, what do you need them to *know* to transform what they *believe*, *feel* and *do*?

If you prepared an objective flow in Chapter 1.2, you'll find it useful here: a new belief, leading to a new feeling, leading to a new action. The Audience Transformation Roadmap expands on this and contrasts it with a more complete understanding of where the audience is before your presentation, so you can work out how to transform them.

When you use the Audience Transformation Roadmap to brainstorm for one of your upcoming presentations, you will realize that a large part of the transformation you need to generate is in the "feeling" and "doing" areas. Without performing this exercise, most presenters focus at least 90% of their energy on the "knowing" part – on telling them facts – where presentations are least effective.

Believing versus feeling

The first time you use the Audience Transformation Roadmap, you might be slightly confused about the distinction between the "believe" and the "feel" boxes. What's the difference between believing and feeling?

A belief is something you think you know or you suspect is likely to be true – or want to be true – whereas a feeling is an emotion that may be caused or triggered by beliefs. The following table features examples of both to show the difference:

Beliefs and feelings

Belief	Feeling
I think my job is at risk.	I feel apprehensive.
I think this is a great company to work for.	I feel enthusiastic and motivated.
I believe my board can make this company grow.	I feel optimistic.
I believe my boss was wrong to criticize me in public.	I feel angry and betrayed.
I think it must be time for lunch.	I feel hungry.

Believing versus knowing

While you will replace "before" actions with "after" actions, and "before" feelings with "after" feelings, you might need to replace some things your audience *believes* beforehand with something they *know* afterwards.

A prior belief may be something they falsely believe they know, and which you need to correct. Perhaps, before you speak, they *believe* you will be announcing a headcount reduction, and you need to ensure they *know* afterwards that in fact you are planning to increase the workforce this year.

Other beliefs will need to be replaced with new beliefs, particularly those which are judgments or predictions. Before you speak, your audience may believe this will be a tough year, and you might want them to believe instead that this promises to be a great year.

Example roadmap

Let's take a quick look at how the Audience Transformation Roadmap works, using an example from the world of sales.

Imagine that our customer had a three-year services contract with us, and that contract will be expiring in a few months.

▶ **What do they know?** They know our company's strengths and weaknesses, and what is in the current contract. They might not know the new services we could offer in a new contract.

▶ **What do they believe?** They believe that by renewing the contract, they're going to get "more of the same" for three years, with all the familiar positive points but also all the usual difficulties.

▶ **What do they feel?** They might feel like they want a change: curious, bored or jaded.

▶ **What do they do?** Most likely, they are preparing an RFP to choose the next supplier, giving our competitors a chance to take our customer away.

Once we've got a clear idea of what the customer knows, believes, feels and does before our presentation, we have to work out what needs to change. What do we want them to know, believe, feel and do *after* our presentation?

Remember: it usually works best to answer these in reverse order, starting at the bottom right of the Roadmap:

▶ **Do:** We want them to forget about the RFP and instead sign a new contract with us.

▶ **Feel:** Before, they felt like they needed a change. We need them to feel happy and enthusiastic about renewing our contract.

▶ **Believe:** Before, they believed that a renewal would be "more of the same". After our presentation, we need them to believe that a new contract will be different, offering more value for money than before.

▶ **Know:** After our presentation, they will need to know that we've developed new services and capabilities since they signed with us three years ago – and they will need to know what's in our new offer, so they can accept and sign it.

The Transformation Column

Now that we have a clear "before" and "after" state for each of the four points in our roadmap and we know how we need to transform our customers, it's time to plot how to make those changes.

This is where the middle column comes in: the Transformation Column. If you've drawn the Audience Transformation Roadmap on a flipchart or whiteboard, once you've filled in the "Before" and "After" columns, take some sticky notes and brainstorm ideas to fill in the Transformation Column.

An idea can be something you might want to say, an example, a story, a reference, a question you might want to ask your audience, a strong image (visual or described), a video or demonstration, or anything else that might generate the transformation you identified between "before" and "after." Use one sticky note per idea.

As you fill in your Transformation Column, aim to include the first two magic ingredients: the audience and yourself. Try to think of ways to speak about the audience and their situation, to bring them into the presentation as active participants wherever possible, and to build in something of yourself: what you feel, what you believe, why you care and stories from your own experience.

In this contract renewal example, we will need to tell the customer about our new services. We could just present our offer, but presenting a solution without first explaining the problem it will solve is like trying to plant a tree without first digging a hole. We could start by asking them about the problems that our new services address to see whether they've experienced those problems and to make them care about our services. We could also give an example of another company that had those problems and then implemented our new services to fix them. That's more memorable and impactful than just telling them what you have to sell. More on this topic in the Creation stage (Section 3).

Once the customer knows about these new services and how they can help their business, we will need to make it clear that our offer will give them better value for money than before, make them believe that they are going to get something new without changing suppliers and feel enthusiastic about it, and persuade them to sign a renewal with us. We will need to give them something to sign and ask them to sign it while also giving them good reasons not to send out an RFP to multiple vendors. We might say, "We're offering you better service at 20% less than before, if you renew early," which helps the buyer convince their internal customers that they've negotiated a better deal, with less work. Most customers who make buying decisions also have internal customers to satisfy – and many procurement specialists don't make final buying decisions, only recommendations to the real decision-makers, so you have to make them want to sell your value proposition as much as buy it.

You should not underestimate the importance of what the customer feels. Even if you make a fantastic offer, if they don't want to keep working with your company or with you personally, they might see an RFP as a chance to find a nicer vendor to work with, knowing that if they don't find one, you'll probably make an even better offer in response to a competitive RFP anyway. You must ensure that the customer always wants to work with you, and then they will find rational reasons to do so. This means you should focus more on the bottom half of the Roadmap – what they feel and what they do – than on what they know and believe.

From sticky notes to storyline

It can be a good idea to take a photo of your Audience Transformation Roadmap on your flipchart or whiteboard and share it with the brain-storm participants. I also sometimes type it up afterwards to take the quality of my handwriting out of the equation. This writing-up activity leads in neatly to the incubation step, helping me to organize the ideas and often to make them clearer.

Once you've filled your Transformation Column with sticky notes about how you can change what your audience knows, believes, feels and does, put these sticky notes in a logical order, like stepping-stones, and that will give you a first version of the structure of your presentation.

I encourage you to stay flexible, however, because Section 3 introduces several storyline templates for various situations, and you might find it helpful to choose one of these templates, with or without a little adaptation, and plug your sticky-note story elements into it.

Drinking our own champagne

You might have heard the expression "to eat your own dog food." This refers to a company using its own products or services – the idea being that you might not have much trust in a tool if its developer never uses it. Although the expression originated from a dog food company, some prefer to say, "to drink our own champagne." Whichever saying you find more palatable, you might be comforted to know that my colleagues and I use the Audience Transformation Roadmap ourselves – not only to brainstorm events and presentations for our clients, but for our own presentations, too.

In 2019, I delivered a talk at TEDxSaclay called "The 3 Magic Ingredients of Amazing Presentations," featuring the three points mentioned at the start of this chapter: the audience, the speaker and the transformation the speaker aims to generate in their audience.[7] The main part of this talk was an explanation of the Audience Transformation Roadmap, using an example. And, applying recursive thinking, I used the Audience Transformation Roadmap to brainstorm for this talk.

In fact, my colleagues and I have used this tool to prepare hundreds of TED(x) talks, thousands of business presentations and more besides.

Beyond presentations

The Audience Transformation Roadmap doesn't only work for presentations: it works for any situation where you need to change what people believe, feel and/or do.

Some of my clients use it to prepare written proposals or important meetings. At Ideas on Stage, we always use it to prepare events and conferences. In fact, I first conceived the Roadmap during a client brainstorm for a conference for the European team of medical directors at a leading healthcare company.

When using the Audience Transformation Roadmap to imagine a meeting or conference, you will likely find that, rather than having one idea per sticky note in the Transformation Column, you instead have one agenda item per sticky note – a presentation, an exercise, a workshop, a team-building activity, etc.

To inspire the audience, we might bring in a motivational speaker; to generate action, we could have a powerful closing keynote from the

CEO. Then, when working with the CEO on their conclusion, we would usually run another brainstorm, referring back to the overall Roadmap and the rest of the agenda as important inputs, and in this new brainstorm we would have one idea, message or story per sticky note, as with any presentation.

When to invest the time

In business, time is money; in fact, for many business leaders, time is scarcer than money. It can take an hour or two to run a complete brainstorming session using the Audience Transformation Roadmap – is it always necessary?

No, not always. For simple presentations where you don't have much preparation time and where your objectives are obvious, you might choose not to use this tool. I don't use it myself for every presentation I give. It is an investment, and, like any business investment, the likely return needs to justify that investment.

But when the stakes are high, and the quality of your presentation may be the difference between success and failure, the Audience Transformation Roadmap is a worthwhile investment, and it can sometimes even be a shortcut. Even I have been amazed when working with clients and seeing them take their ideas from the Transformation Column, arrange them in a suitable order, and say "Wow!" when they realize that the resulting storyline is exactly what they need to say – no more, no less.

 Try the Audience Transformation Roadmap for your next important presentation – and you might be the one saying "Wow!"

2.3
IDEATION: SUMMARY AND ACTION STEPS

Now you have an overview of the creative process and you have discovered the Audience Transformation Roadmap, it's time to put these techniques to work on your own presentation, building on the foundation you prepared in Section 1.

1. **Research:** Spend some time researching your audience and the subject, using available online resources and asking anyone with useful knowledge or contacts.

2. **Brainstorm:** Draw the Audience Transformation Roadmap on a flipchart or whiteboard, or use the template available for download from **bpr-book.com**. If you can gather a small group of colleagues for steps 3-5, you'll find the exercise even more powerful.

3. Fill in the "Before" column of the Roadmap, starting from the top, working out what relevant things the audience knows, believes, feels and does before your talk.

4. Fill in the "After" column, starting from the bottom, working out what you want the audience to do, feel, believe and know after the presentation.

5. Brainstorm ideas for making those transformations, filling in the middle "Transformation Column" with sticky notes.

6. **Incubate:** Let your ideas incubate in your subconscious mind, at least overnight, but ideally for a day or so.

7. **Output:** Perform steps 3-5 again without looking at what you did before. See what new ideas you came up with.

8. Look back at your first Audience Transformation Roadmap and compare it with the new one. Put your "old" and "new" transformation ideas together, discarding any doubles.

Even if you don't have time to complete steps 6-8, you should end up with an interesting set of ideas that you can work into your storyline in the Creation stage.

Preparing to succeed

The Foundation and Ideation stages will set you up for success if you take the time to complete them; yet, most presenters don't make the effort. If your objectives are worth taking time to present to your audience, they are also worth the preparation time.

Here is a recap of the key steps in the pSCORE process that we've covered so far:

1. Start with ABC: who is your audience, what are their burning needs and what is the context?

2. Choose your objectives: how do you aim to transform your audience? "After this presentation, the audience will…"

3. Follow the four steps of the creative process: Research, Brainstorm, Incubate and Output. This will help you generate ideas for what you might say and show during your presentation.

4. Use the Audience Transformation Roadmap as a brainstorm canvas to chart the changes you need to make in what your audience

knows, believes, feels and does, and to think of what you could say and show to achieve those transformations.

Now you have laid this foundation and identified the ingredients of your presentation, it's time to create your storyline in a way that awakens your audience's interest, keeps their attention and communicates your key messages memorably.

3 CREATION

Prepare your storyline
before your slides.

3.1
WHY STORY?

Now that we understand our audience, their burning needs and the context, and now that we have transformational objectives and plenty of ideas for what we might say to achieve those objectives, it's time to put these elements together and create our presentation.

This doesn't mean slides – at least, not yet. What it means is story.

This section takes the art of storytelling and applies it to creating business presentations, using the techniques of screenwriters and playwrights to capture attention, keep people listening, and communicate messages clearly, effectively and memorably.

By the end of this section, you'll know exactly what you plan to say, and you'll be ready to illustrate it with slides if and where they help your audience. Remember: a successful presentation is not one where a speaker comments on slides but where the slides illustrate and reinforce the speaker's messages.

Resist the temptation to open PowerPoint and start preparing slides until you have prepared your storyline. This may be a significant change in the way you prepare presentations. It will also make a significant difference to the quality of your presentations.

Don't put the cart before the horse:
first decide what to say,
then think about what to show.

The storytelling animal

You would be forgiven for wondering why a serious business book talks about storytelling. Rest assured: this is not about Cinderella, or even Hamlet. Even if your sales targets have nothing to do with fantasy or your product's advertised features aren't just a fairy-tale, storytelling is the most effective way to get your message across to your audience.

There is an evolutionary reason for this. For the majority of human history, we could neither read nor write – but we could speak and listen. Everything we learned was in the form of stories. Today, scientists know that our brains are wired to enjoy stories, to pay attention to them and to remember them.[8]

If you don't believe me, think of the story of Marie from Section 1. Can you recall it? I'm sure you can. I often tell this story in training courses on day one, including many more details, and then on day two I ask participants to tell us Marie's story. Almost everybody can remember most of the details, even when the second day takes place a whole week later.

By contrast, you might find it hard to remember the five simple words that make up the five key success factors of pSCORE. Can you recall them? (Fear not: we will go through them again in this section, and in the next ones.)

By default, people will forget what you tell them.
Storytelling is a great way to make your messages stick.

The power of story

Here's another example from my past career in sales. Although I was selling multinational print outsourcing contracts, customers often asked me why brand-name toner cartridges cost so much more than generic ones.

At first, I gave the usual answers about the quality of materials, the recy-cling program and the moving parts. These facts and figures rarely satis-fied anyone.

Later, I would answer such questions with a story – a true story, naturally:

> I had just arrived in a procurement director's office in Finland, ready for a long day of contract negotiations, and the day didn't start well because he was an angry man. He showed me a piece of paper with two lines all the way down it: one yellow, and one magenta.

> "Look at this! This comes from your damn color laser printer over there! I end up having to print everything again on another printer in a different office, and that wastes time and money."

> Although I am no technician, I asked whether I could take a look at the printer. As I opened the cartridge door, two things were immediately obvious. The first was that the magenta and yellow cartridges had leaked, and there was toner everywhere. The second was that they were cheap third-party cartridges – whereas the black and cyan cartridges, which hadn't leaked, were our brand.

> I pointed this out to the customer, and I asked him how much it would cost to have the printer cleaned and replace the cartridges, added to the cost of printing many pages twice and the time wasted going to the company's other office to pick up documents.

> Then I paused and asked him whether he was going to keep buying cheap low-quality cartridges. Of course, he realized they were a false economy. He never bought a third-party cartridge again.

No customer who heard that story ever asked about toner prices again. That's the power of story.

Stories within stories

Anecdotes and examples are important communication tools, but there are plenty more in the business presenter's storytelling toolbox.

 Storytelling in business goes way beyond telling stories.

The first responsibility of every presenter is to keep the audience awake and fully attentive. If they are attentive, they are influenceable; and if they are influenceable, they can be transformed. The opposite is also true.

You need to produce an original presentation every time, and that means using the power of story to grab their attention at the start, maintain it all the way through and wrap everything up properly at the end.

There are three main aspects of storytelling in business presentations:

1. **Structure:** think of your presentation as one big story, structured using storytelling techniques.

2. **Anecdotes:** inside that big story, include smaller stories, examples and anecdotes to make your key messages stick.

3. **"Chocolate chips":** while plain cookies can be good, it's the chocolate chips that make them especially enjoyable and moreish. In your presentation, include analogies, surprises, actions and other storytelling techniques to reset your audience's attention and make your presentation more enjoyable.

There is no one perfect presentation recipe, and pSCORE will lead you to different results depending on your audience, your context and many other factors. The aim in this section is to give you the best ingredients, simple presentation cooking techniques and plenty of inspiration. The rest is up to you.

3.2
SCORE WITH STORY

In the introduction to this book, we looked at the five pSCORE success criteria as they apply to our presentation: Simple. Clear. Original. Related. Enjoyable.

These criteria guided us during the Foundation and Ideation stages, ensuring we laid the groundwork for a successful presentation.

In the Creation, Illustration and Connection stages, we can be even more specific by outlining what success looks like using these five criteria. So, before we start preparing our storyline, let's apply the pSCORE success criteria to the Creation stage, using the art of storytelling to build the structure and content of our presentation.

Simple

The first thing to remember is that what you leave out is more important than what you leave in. Say too much, and you will lose your audience's attention – or, even if you keep it, there will be too much information competing for limited space in their memories.

In the Ideation stage, you came up with many ideas and possible things to say. Simplicity says that it may be impossible to include all of them in your presentation and still achieve your objectives.

Imagine that the Ideation stage was like going to the market and buying lots of high-quality fresh food, which is now ready to prepare in your kitchen. You don't need to put everything into a single dish. Likewise, you have a lot of presentation ingredients available to you, but do not expect they will all make it into your storyline.

 Leave out what is not absolutely necessary: the superfluous weakens the essential. The best presentations don't say much but say it well.

Clear

When it comes to presenting, the structure should be clear. No audience likes to feel lost in the middle of a presentation. You might choose to keep one small element of your presentation a surprise, but bear in mind that some business audiences don't like too much surprise, and boardrooms like no surprises at all, ever.

A clear structure always requires a strong introduction that makes people want to listen, and a conclusion that wraps up the presentation together with any call to action. Too many presentations fail simply because there is no conclusion, leaving the audience wondering what they are supposed to remember and do, or even what the point of the presentation was. In most cases, they don't wonder for very long.

Your objective and key messages should also be clear to your audience. If they don't know why you are presenting, what you want them to do or what they should remember, they will neither do nor remember anything.

 A successful presentation needs a clear structure, clear objectives and a few clear messages. If the audience feels lost, nobody wins.

Original

We've already seen that in presentations "typical" and "predictable" are synonyms for "boring," and this message bears repeating because it is important to remember. You should therefore make your storyline unique so the audience remembers it. You could give it a stand-out theme and build the talk around it; for example, Garr Reynolds gave a TEDxTokyo talk about resilience using the theme of bamboo, a tree that bends where others break, and that can therefore resist the strongest storms.[9]

When preparing a corporate event, we aim to give it an original theme and relate every agenda item to that theme in some way. Within that, we will still aim to make every presentation different. When preparing an athletics-themed online kick-off for Boston Scientific, we "covered" ten sporting events, each representing a story, strength or value we wanted to highlight, but we changed the format and style for each "event."

You might not always be able to use an original theme, but sometimes you can use an original structure. When I present about how to speak on stage, I often use the structure of the human body, starting with the feet and working upwards.

 What you choose to say, and in what order, will make your presentation predictable and boring, or original and interesting. If your presentation doesn't stand out, your messages won't sink in.

Related

There are all kinds of wonderful presentation storylines and techniques, but not all of them are appropriate in all circumstances. Choose your techniques carefully. I have had great success using hundreds of balloons and asking audiences to blow them up – but I wouldn't dream of trying to do that in a boardroom during a tough quarter.

While giving a talk at a TED conference, Bill Gates released mosquitoes into the audience to raise awareness of malaria.[10] It was extremely memorable, but it wouldn't be effective for a virtual meeting where audience members were sitting comfortably in their home offices.

There is a time and a place for everything, and just as the presentation's objective and key messages are related to the specific audience and context, the storytelling approach should also be chosen with that audience and context in mind.

Choose your storyline and your "chocolate chips" carefully. What works well in one situation may fall flat in another. If your presentation is not related to your audience and the context, it won't SCORE – and you might end up with an own goal.

Enjoyable

We saw in Chapter 3.1 that presenters have to gain and keep their audience's attention if they are to have any hope of getting through to them, and that making the presentation enjoyable (although not necessarily fun) is necessary.

If you pack your presentation full of boring facts, it will be hard to keep the audience's attention, no matter how engagingly you speak. If you show them graph after graph after graph, it doesn't matter how well-designed they are: your audience will rapidly reach information overload and switch off.

I like to use the analogy of an hourglass. Imagine that the grains of sand are your audience's attention. Before long, the sand will run out – and their attention will drop. It is up to you to say, show or do something to turn the hourglass over and reset their attention.

When it comes to online meetings, the hourglass is smaller: the audience's attention span is considerably shorter. It is hard to keep them listening when you don't know whether they are paying attention – and when they know you don't know – so, when presenting online, you have to work twice as hard to make your presentation enjoyable. The more the audience enjoys it, the more they will listen and remember what you say, and the more positive they will feel about you and your messages.

 It is not up to the audience to make an effort to listen;
it is up to you to be worth listening to.
Design your storyline for effortless attention
and you'll be halfway to success.

Now that we've seen the five success criteria, it's time to start building our storyline and learning the storytelling techniques that will make it SCORE with your audience.

3.3
SIMPLE: CHOOSE YOUR KEY MESSAGES

Some messages are more equal than others

After completing the Audience Transformation Roadmap in Section 2, your flipchart or whiteboard should be tastefully decorated with sticky notes, each representing a potential element of your storyline. Now it's time to ask yourself:

> To achieve your objective(s), what does your audience
> need to remember next week?

This can be a harder question to answer than you might imagine because you need to limit your answer to no more than three things. Human brains have trouble taking in too many things at once, particularly when listening rather than reading, so you will need to exercise restraint.

One way to do this is to look carefully at your sticky notes and choose one, two or three points that are particularly important. Then you will need to find a way to link them, make the audience care, and make them actionable. You can achieve this by producing an "elevator pitch."

The elevator pitch

The idea behind an "elevator pitch" is to imagine you are in an elevator and the CEO (or an investor) walks in and says hello. You have only the time it takes to reach the executive suite to make them interested in your project or idea. Now imagine that you have a stand at a business event, and someone stops and asks what you do. You have only a limited time to make them interested and want to know more – and therefore stay longer at your stand. This means your "elevator pitch" should be no longer than thirty seconds, which gives you about seventy words.

Why create a thirty-second "elevator pitch" when you actually have fifteen minutes for your presentation? Over many hundreds of presentation workshops, I've found that this is the fastest and most effective way to start the Creation stage, and, as you'll see later in this section, it's a handy shortcut.

Your task, at the end of this chapter, will therefore be to write out a seventy-word elevator pitch, imagining that instead of your ten, fifteen or forty-five minutes, you only have thirty seconds to speak to your audience. This elevator pitch is not just an introduction to a longer speech: it is a complete presentation in seventy words.

Please don't think that you now have to throw away all the other ideas you came up with before. It's simply important at this stage to understand what is key and what is secondary. After all, if everything is a priority, nothing is a priority.

What? So what? What next?

In *Presentation Zen*, Garr Reynolds says there are two key questions an audience should be able to answer: what are you saying, and why should they care?[11]

In business presentations, I like to add a third one: what do you expect from them, or what is your call to action?

These questions can be summarized as: "What? So what? What next?"

▶ **What?** What are the key messages they should remember?

▶ **So what?** Why are these messages important to them?

▶ **What next?** Now they understand what you are saying and why it is important to them, what do you need from them?

If you answer these three questions in seventy words, you will end up with a strong elevator pitch, and it will be clear to you what is necessary – and what is superfluous – so you can focus on these key points when building your presentation.

As an example, here's the elevator pitch for a recent one-hour talk I worked on with renowned author and business professor Isaac Getz about altruistic corporations, delivered in front of 250 top executives at a major international company:

> Most corporations serve only their shareholders. Some try to make social and environmental contributions – while still maximizing profits.

> My research shows companies' first priority should instead be engaging their employees. Then they can focus on unconditional care for customers, suppliers, and communities. By doing that, strong financial results naturally follow.

> Your future's at stake, so transform your company to focus on these priorities and, as a result, enjoy sustainable success.

Once we had this elevator pitch, we were able to follow the next steps of the creation process to build a compelling storyline. If you can say it in thirty seconds, you can say it in an hour. If you can't say it in thirty seconds, maybe your message isn't clear enough.

Activities: Choose your key messages

Performing these activities and choosing your most important messages is vital for the next stage as we build our presentation. If it isn't clear to you which messages are key, it certainly won't be clear to your audience; and if they remember anything, it might be completely different from what you intend.

1. Visit **bpr-book.com**, choose a talk from the playlists, and write down all the important messages while you are listening to it.

2. Select three key messages from this talk and produce a thirty-second summary featuring these three key messages. Would the speaker's objectives be fulfilled if you only remembered those three messages one week later?

3. Now, switching to your own presentation, take the results of your brainstorm and/or Audience Transformation Roadmap and choose up to three key messages that the audience must remember one week later for you to achieve your stated transformation objective.

4. Finally, write a thirty-second summary (seventy words or less) of your presentation featuring these key messages and ideally answering the three questions: "What? So what? What next?" Now it should be clear to you what is vital and what is merely nice to have.

By the end of this chapter, you should have a short elevator pitch that covers the "What? So what? What next?" of your presentation: your key messages, why your audience should care and what you expect from them. This will help you to keep your storyline Simple: a few key messages, delivered powerfully and with an aim of transformation, not information.

Now it's time to work on building the storyline for our full presentation, and that means building a Clear and Related structure.

3.4
CLEAR AND RELATED: CREATING YOUR STORYLINE

Baking presentations

It's time to wash our hands, roll up our sleeves and get to work on building our storyline with a clear structure. While there is no one perfect presentation recipe, some ingredients (like stories and chocolate chips) work better than others.

Most cakes use the same basic ingredients like flour, sugar, butter and eggs, yet there are thousands of types of cakes. Sometimes unexpected ingredients can deliver great results. I don't know who first thought of putting carrots in cakes, but it turned out to be an excellent idea.

I am very fond of cakes – one HP sales director even called me The Cake Man – so I'm going to use the analogy of baking cakes to create the storyline of our presentation. Every result will be different, even with the same ingredients, and that's part of the beauty of presentations.

Choose your structure

When planning to bake a cake, one of the first steps is choosing what kind of cake to bake. You don't make a pavlova in the same way you'd make a Victoria sponge.

In the same way, for example, the storylines for an investor pitch and a sales presentation will flow differently. Choosing a Clear structure is important; choosing a Related structure is doubly important.

The simplest structure is also the most widely used: introduction, development, conclusion. In many situations, this works well. There is no need to complicate things when the simple is good enough.

In some cases, you might find it more powerful to choose another structure. At **bpr-book.com**, you will find an outline of many different presentation structures, for everything from a board presentation to a product launch, along with examples. I have made these structures available online in a downloadable format rather than taking up an extra forty pages in this book with them.

Here, though, is one powerful example: Ideal, Reality, Problem, Solution. This is a storyline popularized by Garr Reynolds, and it can fit well in many business situations, especially where you need to convince people to act.[12] You can think of it as:

"Ideal, but Reality, because Problem, so Solution."

1. **Ideal:** Start off with an outline of how things could be in an ideal world, or if a particular problem did not exist.

   For example:

   "Imagine if all business presentations could be so effective and interesting that people would actually enjoy them, listen attentively, and remember all the key messages and action points."

2. **Reality:** Next, explain how – in contrast to the ideal world – the current situation is most definitely not good enough and needs to change.

   For example:

   "Unfortunately, most business presentations fail. They are a waste of precious time, and all people remember is how bored they were."

3. **Problem:** Here is where you get to why the reality is less than ideal.

   For example:

   "The main cause of the presentation problem is that people haven't been trained on business presentation skills or visual communication, and they've been led to believe that bullet points are an effective way of communicating information or generating action – which they are not."

4. **Solution:** This is another element of contrast where we move from the problem to the solution: your recommendation. Explain how you're going to solve the problem and move Reality toward the Ideal you outlined at the start.

   For example:

   "Based on what has worked well in other companies, I recommend a three-point solution:
   - Training people on a new, effective way of presenting would be a worthwhile investment for any company, and we should start training our people as soon as possible.
   - It will take time to get everyone trained, but we're wasting hours every day on poor meetings and presentations, so we should immediately buy a copy of *Business Presentation Revolution* for every employee and ensure they read it and apply the pSCORE method.
   - Management must lead by example with their own presentations, showing what is expected as well as what can be achieved."

5. **Conclusion:** Finally, conclude with a call to action or approval to set the ball rolling for your solution.

   For example:

   "I'd therefore like to have our executives prepare some fantastic short presentations for the next all-employee meeting, with the help of a presentation specialist. Once everyone has seen what our company's future presentations should look like, we'll distribute a copy of *Business Presentation Revolution* to all employees in their goodie-bag at the meeting. Do I have your approval?"

Take a moment now to look through the storyline templates available at **bpr-book.com**, and choose one that you think will suit the presentation you're preparing.

You might decide to adapt the recipe a little to make it fit your presentation better. Perhaps you chose the basic template, but instead of three main ideas you only have two. Or you might choose to combine two storylines – like a carrot-cake cheesecake, this can give unexpected yet amazing results.

Your choices should give you an outline with the appropriate stages of your presentation. Either download the template and open it, or draw your outline in a matrix on a flipchart or whiteboard, from top to bottom, leaving space to put sticky notes in each box to represent each item in your presentation.

Now you have chosen the right tin for your presentation cake, it's time to fill it up with the ingredients you prepared earlier.

Arrange your ingredients

If you completed a brainstorming process with the Audience Transformation Roadmap during the Ideation stage, you should already have plenty of ideas of what to say to achieve your transformational objectives. Those are your ingredients.

You can now take these ingredients and put them into your cake tin – i.e., put each idea or message into the right place in your outline. If you brainstormed on a flipchart or whiteboard, or printed it on a big sheet of paper, this means putting each sticky note (one per idea or message) into the right box.

If you skipped the Audience Transformation Roadmap (as I mentioned, I don't use it myself every time, although I do always identify an objective flow first), you might decide to do your brainstorming now. Fill your empty canvas with ideas for what to say, show and do in each part of the presentation to achieve the transformational objectives you identified earlier. I recommend using sticky notes as before.

Holes and leftovers

It is amazing when you follow this process and find that all your ideas fit perfectly into the outline, with no holes and nothing left over. It's like making the right amount of cake mix to fit the tin exactly.

It doesn't happen every time, though.

Most likely, you will end up with a few ingredients that don't fit anywhere, and you might also have some parts of your storyline that need extra ideas or messages that you didn't think of in the Ideation stage.

You should not try to fit the leftovers into the remaining holes. In the brainstorming step, perhaps you came up with more ideas than you need and more things to say than you have time for. Be ruthless about cutting out everything you don't need.

 The more you say, the less they will remember.
Say only what is necessary to achieve your objectives
and make your key messages stick. In a presentation,
the superfluous weakens the essential.

It's perfectly fine to leave some ideas out. In fact, if you're not, you should be concerned that either your brainstorm wasn't productive enough or you're in danger of saying too much. Remember: to SCORE you need to keep it simple.

On the other hand, you might also find that you need more points to make your presentation flow properly. This is where we realize that being creative does not (and should not) only happen in the Ideation stage. Recall the importance of incubation to the creative process: the earlier you prepare your presentation, the more time you have before the due date to think of new ideas to improve it.

At this point, if you still have holes in your storyline and you feel you need to add some points, think creatively, remembering your transformational objectives, and you'll likely find the right elements to add to your storyline. Sometimes it's the dash of rum or lemon juice that you add at the last minute that makes the cake special.

Summary and activities: Creating your storyline

A Clear structure is the backbone of a strong presentation. If your ideas flow naturally, your storyline is Related to the context and your objectives and your audience never feels lost, you will find it far easier to keep their attention. Remember that the word "storyline" is not chosen randomly: your presentation should follow a cohesive narrative, instead of being a collection of randomly arranged points.

Here's a summary of the steps to build the storyline for your next presentation:

1. Choose one of the storyline templates from **bpr-book.com**, and adapt it a little if required to fit your needs.

2. Draw the outline on a flipchart or whiteboard, and then fill in the ideas and story elements from your brainstorming, ideally on sticky notes, arranging them on your template until you are happy with the order.

3. Discard any ideas or messages that don't fit or that you don't need, and fill in any blanks that your brainstorming didn't provide.

By the end of this chapter, to communicate your Simple messages, you should have a Clear and Related storyline using a structure that suits your objectives, your audience, their needs and the context.

That's great, as far as it goes. Simple, Clear and Related are necessary, but not sufficient, to keep people's attention. Next, we're going to add icing to your cake, or chocolate chips to your cookies, and make this storyline Original and Enjoyable.

3.5

ORIGINAL AND ENJOYABLE: DESIGNING FOR ATTENTION

Cookies need chocolate chips

Your audience will forget most of what you say. This is why we focus on no more than three key messages, but even they will be quickly forgotten unless you find a way to make them stick. This means each key message needs to be memorable, but your whole presentation needs to be memorable, too.

Continuing the analogy of baking a cake, so far you might have a perfectly recognizable and edible cake, but it may be a little bland. Your presentation storyline might be Clear and Related, but it might need a little something extra to make it stand out, turn over the audience's attention hourglass regularly, and make your key messages memorable.

This is where we move to the second and third parts of business storytelling: making the storyline Original and Enjoyable with anecdotes and chocolate chips.

Anecdotes and examples

We've already seen in this section that we remember stories, and I've been using examples and anecdotes all through this book to make my messages stick. You can do that in your presentations, too.

Crucially, these stories all include enough detail to make the story seem real, helping the reader to visualize it and remember it. How many ugly slides did the cosmetics company show? What color were the leaking toner cartridges? You can probably answer these questions, and that shouldn't surprise you because you read the details in the form of stories.

These details also have something in common: they are completely irrelevant to the key messages I was trying to convey. However, they help you to remember the story and the key message behind the story; therefore, they are useful details.

 Tell stories with enough detail that they can easily be visualized, and your audience will pay attention, remember them and remember the key messages behind them.

An emotional ride

The best way to your audience's memory is often through their emotions. Perhaps you want to create positive emotions by being amusing, although be aware that using humor is a high-risk strategy in most business situations. The reward can be great if you do it well, but you can lose credibility if you attempt to be funny but fail or if you misjudge the context and make a joke or witty comment at the wrong time.

You can also use negative emotions like fear or shock, but use them carefully, especially in board meetings. If you use a negative emotion, be sure to contrast it with a positive one afterwards: if you show a problem, follow it with a potential solution.

Surprise is one effective emotion. Nobody expected Bill Gates to release those mosquitoes into the TED audience – but everybody who was there remembered it, and it certainly turned over the hourglass of their attention.

You could also elicit compassion. We were proud to work with Dr. Shelly Batra for her TEDxWBG (World Bank Group) talk in 2014, which she began by showing a school bag that a young girl no longer needed because she was thrown out of school when she contracted tuberculosis.[13] This made people care right from the start, and it made them want to find out what happened to this poor girl. (Hat tip to my Ideas on Stage colleague, Joe Ross, who did such fine work on Dr. Batra's storyline.)

Resist the temptation to produce a completely serious, emotionless presentation. Remember that feelings lead to actions, so make sure you are provoking some emotion (other than boredom) regularly during your presentation.

 Creating an emotional reaction is the key to the audience's attention: if they feel nothing, they won't feel like listening. Emotion is a hook on which you can hang your messages.

MAGIQ Moments

If you've diligently performed all the activities in this book so far, you'll have watched several presentation videos. What do you remember most from them?

When launching the MacBook Air, Steve Jobs pulled his ultra-thin computer out of an envelope. This was far more memorable than just telling the audience how thin it was compared to competitor devices.

In a TED talk, Jamie Oliver showed how much sugar schoolchildren ingest while drinking sweetened milk at school, not with a graph but by emptying a wheelbarrow of sugar cubes onto the stage.[14] (At this point, my insurance agent would like me to point out that I am not recommending the release of biting insects or the emptying of wheelbarrows at your next sales meeting.)

These actions are particularly memorable. I call them MAGIQ Moments: they Make A Great Impression Quickly.

MAGIQ Moments don't always involve a physical action. An inventive and unexpected slide, or something you say, can work just as well. When

Jobs launched the iPhone, he announced three major revolutions equivalent in importance to the Mac and the iPod – and then surprised everyone by saying that instead of the three products they expected, he was launching the three revolutions in a single device.[15]

On the *Business Presentation Revolution* website, you'll find a playlist of videos that include exceptional MAGIQ Moments.

What do these MAGIQ Moments have in common? They are things you say, show or do that are unexpected and ideally unprecedented: something the viewer has never seen or heard before.

 If you build a MAGIQ Moment into your presentation, it will stay in the audience's memory longer than any facts or figures – and it will help them remember your key messages.

The icing on the cake

Imagine there are ten other pastry chefs like you making similar cakes on the same day. How do you make yours stand out?

Just as you might decorate a cake and give it a theme, you might want to have an interesting concept running through your presentation that makes it different, makes it stand out and makes it stick. A concept turns a good presentation into a high-impact, memorable presentation, just as football-field icing can turn a basic chocolate sponge into a memorable birthday cake.

I once wrote and produced a two-day event for a French company using the theme of a space voyage. For a financial services company, we produced a customer experience presentation using the theme of pizza delivery. A recent client presented a three-year business plan as a "triple jump," with associated imagery and analogies, and nobody is going to forget this presentation any time soon. How many business plans or strategy presentations are that memorable?

In this section, I've used the concept of baking cakes to make the presen-tation creation process more interesting, and chocolate chips to represent the special ingredients that will make your presentation more original and enjoyable and turn over the hourglass of your audience's attention (yet another analogy).

Analogies and themes work. If you decide to produce a presentation with neither, at least make it a conscious decision and use enough other techniques to make your messages memorable.

Activities: Designing for attention

Now we come back to the Clear and Related storyline you produced and add those anecdotes and chocolate chips to make it Original and Enjoyable.

1. Think back to all the online talks you've watched while reading Section 3 (if you haven't watched any yet, do so now using the playlists at **bpr-book.com**). What do you remember from these talks? What were their key messages? How did the presenters make each key message stick?

2. Look back at the presentation storyline you produced in Chapter 3.4. Look for a concept or theme that can run through your presentation and make it more original and memorable for your audience. If you find one, adjust your storyline so the concept runs through from start to finish without being overpowering.

3. For each of the key messages you want to convey, try to find an anecdote, analogy, or MAGIQ Moment that will help your audience remember it and build it into your storyline.

4. Rehearse your storyline and see whether it all works, and modify it if needed.

Now that you have the flow in some detail, it's time to create the two most important layers of your cake: the base (the conclusion) and the topping (the introduction).

If you're baking a cheesecake, you'll need to prepare the base first, even though it forms the bottom of the cake. When preparing presentations, I likewise recommend preparing your conclusion first. In fact, perhaps without realizing it, that's what you've already done – as you'll discover in the next chapter.

3.6
LAST IMPRESSIONS FIRST

The two-headed match

Imagine that your presentation is a match (the kind you use to light a fire, not the kind that causes normal people to develop a sudden hatred for anyone wearing a different team's shirt).

When you strike a match, it bursts into life. Then it keeps burning… until it flickers and dies. If that describes your presentation, then it's better than most presentations because at least it starts powerfully and makes people want to listen. But it doesn't have a strong conclusion.

This is a major problem with typical business presentations, yet it is the easiest thing to fix: simply assume that by the time you reach the end, the audience has forgotten what you said and will only remember if you remind them.

 Your conclusion is half the value of your presentation. If you don't deliver a strong conclusion, you might as well not bother covering the rest because the audience will forget it.

Imagine, now, that your match has two heads, one at each end. When you strike it, it bursts into life as before. It keeps burning as before. But when it comes to the end, it reaches the second head, and, like a firework, it bursts into life again. This is like a presentation that ends as powerfully as it begins.

The introduction and conclusion are the two most important parts of your presentation. Your introduction should make them want to listen, and your conclusion should make them want to act.

Start at the finish

When helping a business leader with a presentation, I always work on the conclusion first, and while this may seem odd, it's an important part of the pSCORE method.

Imagine that your presentation is like a journey – from A to B, from where your audience is to where you need to take them, from the introduction to the conclusion.

When you use a satellite navigation system or route mapping app, you tell it where you want to go, and it finds the best route to take you there. When I am preparing a presentation, I start with the destination – the conclusion – because when I know where we need to go, I can find a good way to get there. If I don't know where I'm going, I'm likely to get lost.

At this point, you're probably wondering why we didn't produce the conclusion before working on the rest of the storyline. Guess what: you already have your conclusion – or at least a first draft of it.

The three tasks of your conclusion

A good conclusion will cover three points:

1. **Remind the audience of your key messages** (What?)

2. **Make them care** (So what?)

3. **Call to action** (What next?)

This should sound familiar to you, because those are the points we covered in our "elevator pitch" in Chapter 3.3. Preparing that seventy-word concentrated version of your presentation helped you identify your key messages, and it also produced a first draft of your conclusion. If your presentation is longer than ten minutes, your conclusion might need to be longer than thirty seconds, but you can use your elevator pitch as a basis for it.

Let's take a look at each of the three points above and ensure they are properly adapted to your presentation's conclusion.

What?

At the start of your conclusion, it's a good idea to signal to your audience that you're coming to a close. Nothing gets the audience's attention back to its top level more effectively than the words: "In conclusion…" or "Let me sum up…"

Next, remind them of your presentation's key points. If you don't, your audience is likely to forget them. Your conclusion is your last opportunity to tell them your key messages and give them a chance to remember them. If you don't clarify what you want them to remember, they may only recall your creased suit and the piece of lettuce stuck between your teeth.

So what?

Put yourself in your audience's shoes. Once they've heard you repeat your key messages, their next unspoken questions will be: "So what? Why should I care? What does this mean for me?"

If those questions are unanswered at the end of your presentation, then the audience won't care and won't change. That's why it is vital to show your audience why they, specifically, should care. You're not presenting for your own benefit: you're presenting for them.

Remember the R in pSCORE: unless your messages are directly Related to your audience and important to them, they will be quickly forgotten.

The "So what?" part of the conclusion is where you make it clear that you're presenting not for your own benefit but for your audience's, and you make it clear what that benefit is.

What next?

If you're giving a sales presentation to a potential customer, you must leave them with a clear call to action, and it should be an action they can accept immediately.

In some cases, it is good to make an audience reflect and come to their own conclusions. With many conference presentations, it can be effective for people to leave without answers but with a lot of relevant questions. In conferences, you might also want your audience to know how they can contact you, and your call to action could involve telling them why they should contact you and how to reach you.

However, in most business situations it's important to give your audience a clear action they can take. Don't leave them guessing or you might find they do nothing – or do something completely different from what you wanted.

If what you want them to remember, believe, feel or do isn't clear to the audience, it won't happen.

Make them clap

Apart from the introduction, which determines whether or not people listen to your presentation, the last line is the one that can make the biggest difference to how they remember it.

In most meeting rooms and executive committees, and most online meetings, you will not get a round of applause. You can cover your "What? So what? What next" and then finish with something a little stronger than "So, er, any questions?" For example:

> "Those are my key points for this morning. Now, I'm sure you have questions. Who's first?"

> "Now I'd like to hear your point of view."

> "That's the end of my presentation, and now I'd like to discuss these three points with you all."

If, however, you are in front of a large audience, you should conclude in a way that makes them want to clap. Here is a simple formula:

1. **A powerful, "tweetable" last line.**

2. **The magic words: "Thank you."**

When you say, "Thank you," the audience understands: "I've finished – please clap now." But it's the powerful last line that will make them want to clap enthusiastically. Let's take a look at some examples.

Example conclusions

I thoroughly enjoyed working with Dr. Alexandre Marchac on his TEDxESCP talk several years ago, aiming to change how people see plastic surgery. His message was that plastic surgery is a cutting-edge science and that it's most useful when it helps people with disfigurations or reconstructs breasts after a mastectomy.

Here's how he made us care *and* clap at the end, after providing three strong examples of innovation in plastic surgery:

What I want you to remember is that plastic surgery isn't just about making people look prettier: it's about changing lives.

And if some normal people dream of plastic surgery to look exceptional, there are also some exceptional people who dream of plastic surgery to become normal – and that's where we can really make a difference.

Thank you.[16]

That last line summed up the whole talk and turned the conventional wisdom about plastic surgery on its head. It was "tweetable" – something short, strong and worth sharing on its own. And he remembered the magic words: "Thank you."

Here's another example, from the conclusion of my first talk at WikiStage, "What are the secrets of a great WikiTalk?":

[What and What next?] If you get the chance to make a WikiTalk, then prepare it properly, use the power of storytelling, speak passionately, and use great visuals.

[So what?] And then not only will you be as effective and as interesting as any movie, you will also get a huge round of applause, and more importantly, through your audience, you really can change the world.

Thank you.[17]

If you hadn't yet seen this talk, just by hearing the conclusion you would understand what my key messages were, why the audience should care and what my call to action was. The same should be true of any conclusion.

If you end up with only one minute for your presentation instead of ten, give them the conclusion. That should be a lot better than nothing.

Activities: Last impressions first

Now it's time for you to finalize the conclusion for your presentation, after a little background research.

1. First, watch some presentations from the curated playlist of talks with great conclusions on **bpr-book.com**. Ask yourself how much you remember after an hour or so.

2. Now, take another look at the "elevator pitch" you prepared in Chapter 3.3. Try to insert it at the end of your presentation's storyline and see how it works as a conclusion.

3. If necessary, refine it, add some sentences for clarity, and make it fit better with the themes or analogies you chose to use, taking care not to make the conclusion too long.

4. Even if you're going to deliver this presentation in an online meeting, or to a few people who are unlikely to clap, try to give it a "tweetable" last line that will make everybody feel positive as you finish speaking.

5. Rehearse your conclusion, perhaps with a colleague, and test how powerful it is. Does it make people want to clap? More importantly, does it make them want to act according to your transformational objectives? If not, rework it and try again.

Now you have finalized your conclusion, it's time to come back to the beginning and create an introduction that will grab the audience's attention right from the start.

3.7
MAKE THEM LISTEN

Thirty seconds to grab them

A venture capitalist once told me that when watching a start-up pitch, he would reach a decision within thirty seconds – not about whether to invest but about whether to keep listening.

This is increasingly true in business presentations because attention spans are getting shorter, and we are less and less tolerant of boring presentations. The explosion of online meetings has accelerated this trend: it's harder than ever to keep people's attention, and therefore more important than ever to grab an audience and make them want to listen, right at the start of your presentation.

Sadly, most presenters use those precious first few seconds to introduce themselves and the presentation's agenda. You might as well start by saying: "Hi, my name's Phil, and here's how I'm going to bore you to death."

If you don't make your audience interested in listening right at the start, they probably won't. If their first impression is that you are going to bore them senseless, their survival instinct will kick in and they will decide to do something less boring instead. Like checking email. Or the cricket score. Or examining the inside of their eyelids.

The audience's attention is critical to the success of your talk. Your introduction is the first thing they'll hear – and if it's not good enough, it might be the last.

Start with emotions

If the first minute of your presentation tells your audience what you're planning to say and why you're a credible voice on the subject, that's great – but all that counts for nothing if they have no wish to listen.

In that case, your introduction failed.

If, however, the audience has no idea what you are going to talk about, and no idea who you are or why you are a credible speaker, but they want to listen to you, then you succeeded.

Making the audience feel like listening is necessary. The rest is just nice to have. The most important word here is the word "feel." Choosing to pay attention is not a rational decision: it's an emotional choice based on how you make them feel.

Continuing the cake analogy, your introduction is like the icing on a cake. Nobody chooses to eat a cake because of the base: what they see first is the icing, and that makes them want to eat it – or not – even if they have no idea what kind of cake is underneath the topping. It's an emotional decision. Likewise, your introduction will make them feel they want to listen – or not – even if they have no idea what you're going to speak about.

To make your audience want to listen, make them feel something in the first thirty seconds of your presentation. Curiosity is a great feeling to provoke; surprise and shock can be equally powerful.

I once began a sales pitch to a chief information officer by telling him that his company was wasting $50,000 every single day. He was shocked and asked me how – he was listening.

One of the most memorable pitches I saw was from Agorize. It began with an unexpected photo of pizzas and the explanation of how the team met while running a student project for a pizza company – and then realized the world needed a marketplace for linking companies with students to run this kind of project. Everybody remembered the pizzas, and thus the story, and thus the start-up's value proposition.

> *Creating an emotional reaction is the key to the audience's attention. If they feel nothing, they won't feel like listening. If they feel a desire to listen, then you've achieved the main aim of your introduction.*

What about the agenda?

Having a clear structure is important for you, but it's vital for your audience. You don't want to let them get lost and wonder where they are in your presentation.

Speakers often show an agenda at the beginning. I recommend doing this after you have already grabbed their attention by producing an emotional reaction because nobody reacts emotionally to an agenda, except to groan in resignation.

In my Business Presentation Revolution training courses, I always start by ensuring the participants understand why most presentations fail, and how successful presentations can be a competitive advantage for them. By the time I explain how the course will take them through the five stages of pSCORE, I already have their attention.

> *Your introduction should arouse their interest; then, if appropriate, show an agenda and explain how you are going to satisfy their interest.*

Activities: Make them listen

Before you finalize the introduction to your presentation, look at some examples and see what works best.

1. Watch some online presentations from the playlist of "presentations with powerful introductions" on **bpr-book.com**.

2. Stop each one after a minute or two and ask yourself:
   - Do you know what the speaker is going to talk about?
   - Do you want to listen?

   If your answers are "Yes" and "No," then either you are not part of the target audience or the introduction failed. If your answers are "No" and "Yes," then the introduction succeeded. If you answered "Yes" to both questions, so much the better. In any case, making the audience want to listen is the key success factor for the introduction.

3. Now, prepare an introduction for your presentation. Look first at what you already have at the beginning of your storyline. You might not need to add anything. If you chose the "Ideal-Reality-Problem-Solution" structure, the "Ideal" content often serves as a good introduction.

   You might need to modify your introduction to ensure you are creating an emotional reaction or you might need to add an introduction before the main part of your storyline begins. In my experience, the initial brainstorm does not always give the best idea for an introduction, so this step can be important. I always find it is easier to add an introduction once the rest of the storyline is clear – this is why (perhaps surprisingly) finalizing your introduction is the last step of the storyline creation process. It's like writing a book and writing the abstract or blurb that goes on the cover last.

   Remember to grab their attention first, and then – if it will help the audience – explain the structure of your presentation.

3.8
CREATION: SUMMARY

Now you have your final storyline, with a strong introduction, a powerful conclusion, a clear and suitable structure, some anecdotes and other "chocolate chips," and perhaps a theme or concept.

Your storyline should achieve all the pSCORE key success factors:

▶ **Simple:** It should be as short as possible, and only as long as is necessary, to achieve your objectives.

▶ **Clear:** It should have a clear structure that fits your presentation's context and objectives.

▶ **Original:** It should offer something new that will make people listen more, featuring one or more anecdotes, if possible, ideally from your own experience.

▶ **Related:** Although the presentation is already related to your audience because you built it around them and the transformations you need to generate in them, it's important that the style and structure of your presentation are related to the context.

▶ **Enjoyable:** It should be the kind of storyline that grabs the audience's attention right away and makes them want to keep listening, turning over the hourglass of their attention regularly.

Before you move on to Section 4 and illustrate your presentation with visual aids, you could flesh out your storyline and write out the whole speech. The shorter your presentation, the more useful (and practical) it is to write it all out, even if you don't stick to it word for word. Aim to speak no faster than 130 words per minute.

 It is better to leave your audience with questions than to tell them too much or to overrun. If you're worried that you have too much content, you probably do.

Let's conclude the Creation stage with a recap of the pSCORE method for producing your storyline:

1. **Simple**: After completing the Foundation and Ideation phases, create a seventy-word "elevator pitch," answering the questions: "What? So what? What next?" This will help you identify your key messages and provides a good first draft of your conclusion.

2. **Clear and Related**: Choose a structure that suits your objectives and the ABC of your presentation.

3. Take the content ideas from your Ideation brainstorm and plug them into the structure you chose. Discard what you don't need and fill in any gaps.

4. **Original and Enjoyable**: If you wish, build in a concept or theme that makes the presentation more memorable.

5. Include some anecdotes or examples to make your key messages stick and keep your audience's attention.

6. Wake up your audience and turn over the hourglass of their attention with a **MAGIQ Moment**: something you say, show or do that Makes A Great Impression Quickly.

7. Use your **elevator pitch** as the basis for a conclusion that reminds your audience of your key messages, explains why they are

important and relevant to them, and tells them what you want them to remember, believe, feel and/or do afterwards: the "What?" the "So what?" and the "What next?"

8. If you have a big enough audience, prepare a powerful last line and finish with a simple "Thank you" to make them want to clap and to give them their cue.

9. Prepare an introduction that creates an emotional reaction in your audience and makes them feel like they want to listen. Then, and only then, consider adding an agenda.

10. Finally, make sure your presentation is a personal talk from you to your audience. If someone else could deliver it, or if you could deliver it to another audience, it's not personal enough.

Following these steps will put you way ahead of most presenters and ensure your storyline grabs their attention, and keeps it until the end, communicating your key messages memorably. This matters because attention leads to action, and only an attentive audience can help you achieve your transformational objectives.

If you're creating a new presentation and building it step by step as you move through the chapters, take a moment now to check that you know what you plan to say in your talk from start to finish – and, ideally, run through it fully, aloud, at least once – before you move on to Section 4.

 If there's one thing more powerful than a story, it's a visual story.

4 ILLUSTRATION

Don't confuse **slides** with **documents.**

4.1
SLIDES AND
SLIDEUMENTS

Doctor Visual and Mr. Slide

Slides can be a powerful way of making your messages clearer and more memorable – yet all too often they are an obstacle to communication. In this section, we'll look at why we should think of slides as visual aids, how they are different from documents or handouts, when we should (and should not) use them, and how to produce successful visual aids that help our audiences and make our presentations more effective.

We'll start our slide revolution by getting rid of the greatest evil of the PowerPoint hegemony: the slideument.

The slideument trap

A *slideument* is as bad as it sounds. This term, which I believe was coined by Garr Reynolds, describes a deck of slides that aims to serve as a set of visual aids during a live presentation but also as a document that can be distributed before, during or after the live presentation – a handout.[18]

Humans can't listen and read different things simultaneously: we can only process one linguistic input at a time.[19] So, if a slide features a lot of text and detail, it might make a useful reference document but a terrible visual aid. If you follow my advice and keep your slides simple, with only a few words, they'll be good visual aids but worthless as handouts.

Most people try to do something in the middle and end up with too little text for a useful reference document but too much for a visual aid – 50% slide, 50% document, 0% effective.

 It's great when you can kill two birds with one stone, but slideuments only kill your audience's attention.

This is a typical slide

- This is the first point, but don't worry - there will be plenty more to come
- In fact there is so much text here
  - that it will be necessary to split it up arbitrarily
  - to avoid making this look like a novel
    - and to use tiny text so we can fit it all on the screen
- So, poor audience, you have the difficult choice:
  - listen to me
  - or read all this text (which you're currently doing)
  - or try doing both, which is impossible for humans
    - and you probably have mostly humans in your audience
- So having all this text behind the speaker doesn't help communication – in fact, quite the opposite
  - because there is zero chance you'll remember any of these bullets

---

A typical "title + bullets" slide that stops the audience from listening

Why rock the boat?

Change is hard. Rowing against the tide is hard. When so many of our colleagues are producing slideuments day after day, is it worth the risk of standing out and delivering presentations that are radically different?

If you're happy being average, by all means follow the crowd. If you prefer to be safe than to be noticed, by all means follow the crowd. But when everyone else is delivering ineffective, boring presentations that their audiences hate, does following the crowd make sense? It's like following all the other lemmings off the cliff.

 The fact that most presentations fail gives you the opportunity to rise above the mediocre masses and get yourself noticed.

Slides versus handouts

Before we get into designing slides, it's important to understand how different slides and handouts need to be.

1. **Slides are for projecting; handouts are for printing.**
   For the audience, slides exist only as light projected on a screen for a short period of time, and they should be designed to work well on a projector screen, a flat-screen monitor and/or an online meeting platform. Handouts, on the other hand, need to be designed so they can be printed if necessary.

2. **Slides support an oral speech; handouts replace it.**
   Good slides don't stop the audience from listening; great slides help the audience listen more closely. Handouts, on the other hand, need to be standalone – easy to understand for someone who missed the live presentation or who refers back to the content after they forgot what the presenter said.

3. **Slides are for looking at; handouts are for reading.**
   Slides should be visual, allowing the brain's linguistic processing to focus almost entirely on what the speaker is saying. Handouts, however, are intended for quiet reading: as there is no speaker to listen to, the brain can focus its linguistic processing fully on the document.

4. **Slides feature only key words; handouts have complete sentences and even paragraphs.**
   Visual slides will have a few words in a large font that the audience can see and understand quickly so they can keep listening to the speaker. Handouts may feature full paragraphs so the reader can understand the content without ambiguity.

5. **Slides often have dark backgrounds; handouts usually have white backgrounds.**
   Good slides will often have dark backgrounds to avoid tiring the audience's eyes. Most handouts will have white backgrounds to make them easy to print without spending a fortune on toner or ink.

6. **Slides should avoid "visual pollution"; handouts should feature meta-data.**
   Items like the page number, the date and the author's name are "visual pollution" when projected on a screen, distracting the audience from what they should be looking at. In a handout, they are helpful.

Slides and handouts are so diametrically opposed in their objectives and characteristics that you couldn't imagine trying to do both with one file. Or could you? Take a look at some of your recent slides and ask yourself whether you fell into the slideument trap.

Producing documents in PowerPoint

I am often asked whether it's acceptable to produce documents in PowerPoint. My answer is: yes, as long as you don't try to use them as slides, and as long as you share them as a PDF file. Nancy Duarte even wrote a book about using PowerPoint to write documents: *Slidedocs*.[20] She wrote it using PowerPoint itself, and I thoroughly recommend it.

PowerPoint can be an excellent tool for producing attractive documents, such as proposals. At Ideas on Stage, we often produce document templates in PowerPoint for our clients.

The danger is that, as Descartes might have said if he were alive today: "I slide, therefore I project." As soon as you have a PowerPoint document, you might be tempted to share or project it during a meeting. If you can resist that temptation, and if you remember to save your document as a PDF file before sharing it (to ensure correct formatting and use of fonts), then yes, you can use PowerPoint for documents.

 If you are going to treat PowerPoint as a Swiss Army knife, only use one tool at a time. Trying to prepare a slide which is also a handout will be as unsuccessful as trying to use the corkscrew and blade at the same time, except that your audience will feel the pain.

Now that you know what a slideument is, and why it is so ineffective both as a slide and as a document, let's take a look at how to make effective use of both slides and documents – starting with the documents.

4.2
EFFECTIVE USE OF HANDOUTS

Prepare to be forgotten

We have spent a large part of this book working to make our talk as memorable as possible, so by now shouldn't we expect our audiences to remember everything we say?

As I write this, I am thinking back to a fantastic TEDx event six weeks ago, and checking how much I remember of the talks – at least, those I didn't help write. The answer is not zero, thankfully, but I can remember maybe two or three points from each of these high-quality presentations.

We forget most of what we hear quickly, so you need to take the long view. It's good to ask yourself what the audience should remember after a few days or a week, and focus on those key messages, but you should assume that after a month they will remember nothing at all.

A month later, your attractive visual slides (if they bother to open them) can no longer explain your points and what you need from your audience. Your handouts, however, can.

 Expect that the audience will forget what you say, and give them a standalone document that will remind them of your key points.

Imagine you are going to pitch your start-up to investors. Can you do that without slides? Yes – and often you will pitch without slides because you will be in a corridor, or a bar, or in the break area at an event. Would your stage pitch be more effective with strong slides? Yes, in many cases, but it can also be effective without them.

Now, imagine an investor is curious and wants to know more or wants to discuss your start-up with a colleague who wasn't there. Wouldn't it be wonderful to have a single sheet (perhaps double-sided) that they could take away with them, read afterwards to remind them of who you are and what you do, hand to a colleague for a second opinion, and use to get back in touch with you?

If your objective is to hook them and get a meeting with them, this kind of short handout is powerful; yet, most start-ups spend all their time on their slides, give investors nothing to take away and wonder why they never hear back from them.

 In many business situations, giving people a handout has more long-term value than the short-term benefit provided by slides – even good ones.

Think of slides and handouts like a gift. The slides are the pretty wrapping paper that make the present more enjoyable when it's received and unwrapped – not necessary, but appreciated. The handouts are the gift that remains useful long after the wrapping paper has been thrown away, or the oral presentation forgotten.

The board wants my slides in advance

How often are you asked to send your slides before a meeting? With executive committees, this happens almost all the time. Why? Generally, there are two reasons, and they both aim to reduce the risk of reprisals for the meeting organizer:

1. The organizer wants to ensure there are no surprises during the meeting (boards hate surprises).

2. The organizer wants to ensure anyone invited to present to the board has prepared their presentation.

These are both valid reasons to send a document in advance, but the organizer asks for your slides because they assume (in true pre-revolution style) that you are going to produce slideuments and they don't know any better way.

Based on my experience with the boards of many international corporations, my first recommendation is to send a short textual document instead: one or two pages, or a one-page executive summary with a few pages of annexes in case they want to read more. Most board members will appreciate this. Alternatively, there may be a standard document template that everyone should complete, and the board will be used to this format. If so, respect it – but accept that it is a document, not slides.

If the organizer still insists on seeing your slide deck, produce some visual pSCORE slides that you will project during the meeting, but add detail in the presenter notes, and then print the "notes pages" to a PDF and share that with the organizer. On each page, you will have the slide, usually at the top, and then the presenter notes underneath. That way, the board will get the visual slides, and the textual messages, so they can understand what you're recommending before the meeting far better than with either visual slides or bullet points.

 Revolutions always meet resistance at first. When you provide good handouts, your audience (and bosses) will feel less concerned about your simple visual slides and are more likely to give your new approach a chance. In my experience, when they see how effective this is, they wonder why nobody thought of it before.

Activities: Effective use of handouts

Complete the following activities related to handouts for the presentation you built in Section 3:

1. If you need to deliver anything to the audience before your presentation, try to summarize your key messages in a one-page executive summary (with font size no smaller than 10-point); if the audience needs more detail, add a few more pages, keeping it short enough that they will read it.

2. If it might help your audience to have a short document with the structure and key messages outlined in each section, with space for handwritten notes, print one and distribute it, or share it electronically with participants.

3. Would your audience benefit from having any of your presentation's content on paper instead of straining their eyes on a screen (such as a table of numbers or a project timeline)? If so, prepare them and print them, and consider the distribution of these "in-flight" handouts during your presentation flow.

4. What kind of handout will help your audience remember your key points and desired outcomes after your presentation? Even if you decided not to produce any handouts in the three activities above, you should strongly consider leaving at least one page with your audience so they can refer back to it months later. (If you do not provide this, they will ask for your slides!)

Thinking carefully about your handout strategy will ensure your audience has the information they need at all times: before, during and after your presentation. And by providing this information in your handouts, you will not feel obliged to include it all in your slides, just in case somebody asks.

Now that you know what you are going to distribute, it is time to start thinking about what you are going to show them. And the answer may be "nothing."

4.3
WHEN NOT
TO USE SLIDES

PowerPoint is not the only tool

The widespread use of PowerPoint in corporate communication has led to one major problem: it is now the default way people present. If your boss asks you, "Have you prepared your presentation?" what they really mean is, "Have you prepared your PowerPoint slides?" As a result, presenters automatically assume that they will use PowerPoint slides and do not consider other possibilities.

Now that you have joined the Business Presentation Revolution, you know how important it is to choose what you are going to say before thinking about how you might illustrate it. You should also ask yourself: do I need to illustrate it at all?

I invite you to assume that your talk does not need slides, unless proven otherwise. Sir Ken Robinson's famous TED talk, "Do Schools Kill Creativity?" uses no visual aids other than the images his stories create in our minds, and at the time of writing it is the most-viewed TED talk of all time.[21]

For each point in your presentation, ask yourself: does my audience need any visual aids? If the answer is yes, ask yourself whether you can use a physical action to illustrate what you are saying. This could mean doing something with your hands or an object, like Steve Jobs pulling an iPod Nano from the smallest pocket of his jeans.

People remember what you do better than what you project, even if your slides are great.

If there's no suitable object or action for this point, your next question should be: would a flipchart or whiteboard (or similar modern media like a smartboard) be a good way to illustrate what I am saying? If the answer is no, then and only then should you consider using slides. Since you are giving suitable handouts anyway, you do not need to produce slides for your audience to take away. You only need them if they help make what you are saying easier to understand and/or more memorable.

The key with any tool is knowing when not to use it. If you only have a hammer, you'll treat everything like a nail; if you assume you are going to use PowerPoint, then you restrict yourself to one illustration method when other choices may be better, and the right choice may be no visual aids at all.

It's not all-or-nothing

Before you decide whether or not to use slides, there is another important revolution to bear in mind.

Prior to the Business Presentation Revolution, presenters generally used slides either throughout their whole presentation or (too rarely) not at all. Now, though, you need to understand that it is not a binary choice. There is no rule saying that because you need a graph here and a diagram there, and perhaps a quotation at the end, you therefore need to use slides at all other times during your presentation.

When I am presenting or teaching, I like to mix things up. This resets the audience's attention regularly, as well as allowing me to use the most appropriate medium at all times. Sometimes I show slides. Sometimes I show videos. Sometimes I use a flipchart or whiteboard to conduct an exercise or to draw a diagram. Sometimes I speak with no visual aids at all, which keeps the audience's full attention on me, especially in online meetings where they get to see me in a much bigger window. Sometimes I have the audience perform exercises to help them learn.

Stopping your slides is easy in online meetings: you simply stop sharing your screen and then start again when you next need a visual aid. But with a live audience, what do you do with PowerPoint and the projector while you are using the whiteboard or telling a story?

I project what I call the World's Best Slide – it's a pure black screen. It looks like the projector or screen has been switched off, so the audience pays no attention to it; yet, the next time I need a slide, I can simply click to advance without having to wait while the projector warms up again. For short periods without slides, this works well. (Don't use the World's Best Slide in an online meeting, or people will think there is a technical problem.)

Now that you know you can – and often should – aim to use slides for some parts but not all of your presentation, you can start to consider when slides may be useful.

Activities: When not to use slides

Before you think about preparing slides, look back at the storyline you produced in Section 3 and identify which parts (if any) would be clearer or more memorable with slides.

1. Split your storyline into points or paragraphs, depending on the level of detail you used when creating it. Recall if and when you planned to use short handouts during the presentation, such as for a data table.

2. For each point or paragraph, ask yourself:

   – Can I deliver this point effectively and memorably without illustrations?

   – If not, is there a way to illustrate the point with a physical object or action?

   – If not, would it be best for me to use a flipchart or whiteboard while making this point, or will it be more effective with a slide?

3. Note your choice of illustration medium for each point. At this stage, you don't need to imagine what your slides will contain: the important thing is to identify at which parts of your presentation your audience will benefit from slides.

Now it's time to start thinking about what those slides might look like.

4.4
SCORE: THE FIVE CHARACTERISTICS OF EFFECTIVE SLIDES

Design is everyone's business

Before we start storyboarding to imagine which kind of slides can help your audience, you need to understand the key success factors for slides used to illustrate an oral presentation.

Please bear in mind that this is not a design manual. Many leaders do not produce their own slides, so there would be little point in devoting many pages here to explaining the finer points of typography, positioning and compatible colors. But as a client of slide designers, internal or external, amateur or professional, you need to know what to ask for – and what to expect from them.

To obtain great slides, I suggest you either work with a professional presentation specialist or ensure that whoever produces your slides has read *Slide:ology* by Nancy Duarte or *Presentation Zen Design* by Garr Reynolds.[22] For showing data, *Better Data Visualizations* by Jonathan Schwabish is also a great choice.[23]

If you design your own slides, get one of those books: this section is not designed to replace them but to help you learn what makes a successful slide, imagine the kinds of visual aids you might use and work effectively with a designer. The examples on the *Business Presentation Revolution* website (**bpr-book.com**) can also help you, and you can find visual inspiration in the curated video playlists, especially the one of "presentations with great slides."

Even when someone else is designing your slides – be it your assistant or a specialist designer or presentation agency – you are responsible for how they look and their impact on both your company brand and your personal brand. You should be personally involved in the storyboarding process and give regular feedback on the design.

 What you say is important, but the quality of your visual aids can have a huge positive or negative impact. Telling a great story with ugly slides is like giving somebody expensive jewelry in a supermarket plastic bag.

Unconventional wisdom

Before we learn what makes great slides SCORE, and then start to storyboard and build the slides for your presentation, we first need to forget what we thought business slides should look like and understand that the conventional wisdom about slides isn't at all wise.

I think of slides as "visual aids" for a presentation, and just that semantic change helps clients break out of the typical perception of a slide and focus on what kind of visuals will aid their audience's understanding and recollection of their key messages.

Here are four characteristics of typical business slides that you should take care to avoid:

1. **Full of bullets**
   The right number of bullet points on a slide is not seven. It's not five. It's zero. That's right – zero.

   Bullet points have their place in a written document, where they distinguish a list of points from the main paragraphs of text. You don't have paragraphs on your slides (at least, not from now on), so even if you have a list of a few items you don't need bullets.

Bullets remind your audience of all the previous boring slides they've seen, and that association makes them subconsciously switch off.

2. Too many words

You already know that your audience can't read and listen at the same time, so limit your slides to a few key words so they don't start reading and stop listening. Anything on your screen dilutes the attention they can pay to what you are saying. Dilute their attention as little as possible, and only for a good reason.

3. Title + text = boredom

Once upon a time, a smart software engineer had the idea of adding default slide layouts with boxes marked "Click here to add a title" and "Click here to add text." Presenters around the world obeyed. Audiences hated it. And the smart software engineer probably defended their inadvertent killing of communication by saying something like: "But there are other layouts people could use."

Most people don't use the various layouts available, if indeed they realize they are available: they just stick to the boring, standard "title + text" layout. Of all the layouts in your organization's slide template, this is perhaps the one you should use the least in visual aids: it's not visual, and it doesn't help anyone.

4. Visual pollution

Another major problem with slides is the visual pollution we cram onto them. If you are not going to give your slides to your audience afterwards – because you're giving them a clear handout instead – you no longer need to treat them like documents.

Get rid of anything superfluous, like page numbers, dates, your name and the tiny illegible confidentiality notice. Every extra element on your slides will dilute the audience's attention, which should be largely focused on you and focused a little on the active content of your slides.

SCORE with your slides

After learning that you can't kill two birds with one slideument, that bullets kill audience attention, that too many words spoil the show and that visual pollution shouldn't litter your slides, now it's time to examine the kind of slides that will help your key messages stick. Let's apply each of the five pSCORE presentation success criteria – Simple, Clear, Original, Related and Enjoyable – to these visual aids.

Simple

A simple slide is one that an audience can understand in less than five seconds, allowing them to focus right back on you and what you are saying without wondering what that complicated pie chart is supposed to mean.

In a simple slide, you should not use much text; if the audience has to read it, they stop listening. A few large, commonly used words can be fine: if we understand them quickly, we can keep listening. You should also remove everything you don't need from the slide and ensure the key message is obvious within those first five seconds.

If your slide is simple, then it doesn't need to stay on the screen for minutes at a time. A slide has no duration: it is what you say that takes time. As long as the audience has understood the slide, they won't mind if you move on. I recall a very successful startup investor pitch featuring twenty-eight slides in five minutes. Nobody complained there were too many. You can use many simple slides per minute, if that is the best way to help your audience understand and remember what you are saying.

However, if your slides are just walls of words, or so full that the audience doesn't know where to start, then one slide is one too many.

 Each time you click, the audience should have no more than five seconds' worth of new material to look at and digest – whether it's on a new slide or additional material on the current slide.

Clear

The next key characteristic of great slides is clarity. This means, first of all, that everything should be easy to see for everyone in the audience.

How big should your text be? It depends on the font, the size of the screen, the size of the room, the resolution of the slide and other factors. I therefore propose a simple guideline:

 If you're not sure your text is big enough to be read on a phone screen, it's not big enough.

If your words are easy to read for someone watching on their smartphone, then they should be big enough for the people at the back of most amphitheaters or meeting rooms. So, forget the 14-point text. (Yes, that goes for graph axes and labels too.) And you should also make every other element easy to see on a smartphone. If you plan to show tiny photos of sixteen team members on one slide, you might as well make it an org-chart document which you share but never present.

Contrast is another common problem. If you are pasting a pie chart from Excel into PowerPoint, it may have small black labels on a red or blue piece of pie. While you might be able to read them on your computer screen, they may be impossible to read on a projector screen.

 If you're not sure you have enough contrast, you don't have enough contrast.

The message of the slide should also be unambiguous. It should either ask a clear question or give a clear answer. If the audience spends too long figuring out what the question or answer is, they stop listening.

 If you're not sure your slide's question or answer is clear enough, make it clearer.

Original

Good slides are original. If you show slides people have seen before, they will lose interest. If your slides look too similar to ones they have seen before, that can also be a problem. You can still use a corporate template, though, as long as it isn't full of visual pollution. In fact, for most business presentations you should use a corporate template so your slides look both cohesive and distinctive versus your competitors' slides. Do not, however, use that template as an excuse for producing boring or ugly slides.

 Originality makes your slides – and your key messages – memorable.

Use photos that people haven't seen before. Show data in an original (and clear) way. Use a font that isn't overused.

Stick-figure clip-art was cool and new in 1996, but you should avoid it today. I also suggest you steer clear of the 3D stick figures you see on stock photo sites. They're less ugly but nowhere near the engaging, original and inspiring communication your business should aim to deliver.

Remember this next time you are tempted to insert a photo of people crowding around a computer screen and feigning interest, or a hand-shake in front of a picture of the Earth to represent global collaboration. Audiences have seen them a thousand times, and they don't need or want to see them again.

*Show your audience something they haven't
seen before, and they'll approach each new
slide with interest and anticipation – and
they will certainly be paying attention.*

Related

Simple, Clear and Original slides can be effective, but only if they are Related to what you are saying at the time.

Remember that you are not standing in front of your audience to comment on your slides. Your slides are there to illustrate what you are saying and make it easier to understand, more impactful and/or more memorable for the audience. If your audience has to spend valuable time and brainpower wondering why you are projecting a sunset photo of a tropical beach when talking about your quarterly results, that's time and brainpower that they're not spending listening to you.

This also means you should never show something on your slide that you are not planning to speak about. Do not assume they can read or digest it while you speak about something else.

*Use pictures, graphs and slides themselves only when
they are related to what you are saying when they're
on screen – no matter how pretty your picture is.*

If your slides are Related to what you are saying at the time, you're on the road to success. You should also take care to ensure what you show is Related to your audience, partly in terms of their expectations, and partly in terms of their cultural sensibilities. For example, I avoid using photos of cows when speaking to audiences in India, and I don't use cricketing images in France.

Enjoyable

A slide should be Enjoyable: pleasant to look at and to digest. This is important for four reasons:

1. **Enjoyment leads to attention**
   The more the audience enjoys your presentation, the more attention they will pay, and the greater your chances of influencing and transforming them. Attractive slides will help them feel pleasure while listening to you, switching their attention on where ugly slides would switch it off.

2. **A lasting positive impression**
   The positive emotions that your enjoyable slides help generate will stick in the audience's minds long after they have forgotten the words you spoke. They will have a more positive feeling about you, your message and your company.

3. **Respect for your audience**
   If your slides are well-designed and attractive, the audience will feel that you have shown them respect by putting time into your preparation. Audiences like to feel respected, and they're likely to respect you in return.

4. **A better brand image**
   Your slides are as much a part of your brand's visual identity as your logo, your business card or your website. Make sure every slide looks good enough to appear in a newspaper article about your company. If it doesn't enhance your brand, it needs work.

Making your slides Enjoyable can pay dividends. I worked with a web start-up a few years ago and advised them on their investor pitch, including how to make their slides SCORE more. A couple of months later, a well-known investor proudly proclaimed to a big audience that he'd invested in this start-up, and what convinced him most was that he found their slides attractive and well-designed. He said he felt that if they put the same skills and attention into their web solutions, they had a great chance of success.

Take the time to ensure your slides are visually appealing – they are a major part of your company's visual identity. Don't let yourself down with unattractive slides.

Activities: SCORE with slides

Look at a few slides you recently used to illustrate an oral presentation, and for each one ask yourself:

1. **Simple:** Does each slide follow the five-second rule? Can the audience understand each click's new content in no more than five seconds? If not, think how you could simplify it – perhaps by removing unnecessary elements and/or by splitting one slide into multiple slides.

2. **Clear:** Look at your slides in the slide-sorter (or Light Table) view, with at least nine slides on the screen. Can you easily understand everything?

   Project your slides onto a screen in a big room and stand at the back. Can you clearly see every element on the screen? Is the contrast good enough?

3. **Original:** Does each slide look distinctive? Could the audience refer back to it afterwards just by describing it, and make it clear which slide they mean? If so, you've won half the battle already.

   On the other hand, do any slides use a boring, tired font, a "title + text" layout or a white background? Has the audience seen the pictures before? If the answer to any of these questions is "yes," try to make the slide more original by changing these elements and breaking the audience's association of your slides with the thousands of bad ones they suffered through before.

4. **Related:** Are any elements on your slide unrelated to what you are saying? Is there anything that you don't mention but assume they will read anyway? Are there any images that look pretty but add no meaning?

   If you have any "yes" answers, consider removing or changing these elements to ensure that only the related elements appear on the screen at all times. Consider using builds so that each element appears only when it is useful.

5. **Enjoyable:** Does the slide look well-designed? Ask a colleague if they think it looks good or bad. Would you be happy if this slide appeared in an article about your company? Does it reflect positively on the quality of your products / services?

   If your slide is not enjoyable enough, how could you redesign it to make it look better? If you need inspiration, look at some of the slide examples and descriptions at **bpr-book.com**. You'll understand which design choices we made, and why, and begin to see what makes for successful business slides.

Now that you understand how slides can SCORE with your audience, you might feel torn between a desire to produce and use visual, pSCORE-style slides and your duty to follow your corporate slide template. If you are concerned that successful slides and your company template are mutually exclusive, you will find advice in Chapter 4.6. For now, trust that you will find a way to succeed with (or despite) this template.

In any case, it is not yet time to open PowerPoint or another slideware application. First, we need a storyboard.

4.5
STORYBOARDING

The aim of storyboarding

If you've been preparing a presentation using the steps in this book, at the end of Chapter 4.3 you will have read through the storyline you prepared in Section 3 and decided where your audience might benefit from some visual aids. Now that you've looked at how slides should SCORE in Chapter 4.4, you're ready to look at what kind of visual aids will help your audience at each of these points in your storyline.

Whereas the storyline is mostly textual (imagine the screenplay for a film, or the book for a stage play), the storyboard is visual. By the end of this chapter, you should have a rough sketch of each slide you need to prepare to illustrate your presentation.

A sketch saves time

What's the point of sketching your slides before opening your slide application? And what does it involve?

An architect doesn't just put some bricks on the ground and begin building, and most artists don't just splash paint onto the canvas. They usually draw detailed plans first, and only when they are satisfied with their plans will they begin creating their masterpieces.

Your time is limited, so you might be impatient to get to the slide design step. Bear with me: this is important. You can save yourself time and end up with better slides by first sketching your storyboard.

Most of the time we spend in slide design applications is on thinking, imagining, and then adjusting, redoing, discarding… and not on the actual design. What if we could save time on all these steps? What if you could have fewer ping-pongs with your designer to end up with the result you want? That's what storyboarding gives you.

 You might say: "A sketch in time saves on design."

Delegating design

If you are not designing your own slides, a storyboard is even more important. Too many communication crimes are perpetrated by managers who ask subordinates to prepare their slides, leaving these poor people to prepare something they hope will please their boss and be easy to use, knowing that in many cases their boss will not spend enough time becoming familiar with the slides before the presentation, let alone rehearsing several times.

The result is usually something that is text-heavy and easy for the presenter to read and improvise around but hard for the audience to follow, and completely ineffective as a visual aid.

 Don't be that boss. Effective communication is one of your most important responsibilities.

You can save time and improve quality by asking someone to design your slides, either an internal slide wizard or an external specialist. If you already asked a presentation specialist to assist in the Ideation and Creation phases, they can also help you imagine a suitable storyboard. But you need to check and approve the storyboard before design begins, and you should play an active part in preparing it.

If you are comfortable with the storyboard, the first set of slides will probably be close to what you're looking for, and the second should be just right.

Storyboarding without slideware

There is no single correct way of storyboarding. Experiment, and use whatever works for you. You could use a notepad or sticky notes, or a whiteboard or flipchart. If you have a graphical tablet, you might find this works well for you. I am more creative when I'm not looking at a screen, so I often use pens and sticky notes.

If you are as bad at drawing as I am, you could use text to describe how your slide should look. Sometimes I will take my storyline or script and convert or paste it into a table in my word processor, and add a column for slide ideas. Then, for each point or paragraph, I write down what (if anything) should appear on the screen while I'm saying those words.

Where I already have a clear visual idea for a slide, I sketch it on a sticky note, photograph it with my phone, and incorporate the image into my table with any text-based instructions, opposite the storyline or script. If you are better at drawing than I am, and have a sketch for every slide, add them to your table next to the appropriate part of the storyline.

Never ask a designer to prepare slides without letting them know what you're going to say while each slide is projected: share the storyline or script with them. This word-processor table is a good way of doing so.

Slide categories

Knowing how you are going to capture your storyboard is one thing; imagining what kind of visual aids will help the audience to understand and/or remember each point is another. Think back to the parts of your storyline where you already identified that a slide would be the best kind of visual aid for your audience. For each point, which of the following kinds of slide will help your audience most?

Structure slides

In his book *Better Presentations*, Jonathan Schwabish calls these "scaffolding slides": they don't have any content as such, but they hold the presentation together, giving it visual cohesion and helping the audience know where they are in the flow.[24]

There are several types of structure slides.

- ▶ You might need a **title slide**. Note that it shouldn't always be your first slide: you might have a short emotional introduction that makes people want to listen, and then, when you have their attention, you can outline what you're going to give them. This can be the appropriate time to show your title slide.

- ▶ **Agenda slides** are helpful in business presentations, as long as you show them regularly. If you have a thirty-minute presentation with five main sections, like most presenters you will probably explain the structure near the beginning. Unlike most presenters, you should also show the agenda at the end of each section so the audience always knows where they are, highlighting the section you're about to begin.

- ▶ Within a section, you might want to speak about several points, without needing visual aids for all of them. You could use a **visual pause**: show the World's Best Slide, or simply stop sharing your slides until you need them again. Alternatively, you could use an **anchor slide:** show a few words and/or an image or icon representing a point as you speak about it. This gives the audience a visual and/or textual representation of what you're saying as well as what you've just said, anchoring their attention and ensuring they don't feel lost.

- ▶ At the end of a section, it can be helpful to include a **recap slide** reminding your audience of your last few points to help them remember them. If you didn't plan such a recap in your storyline, there's still time to add it.

Training Course Agenda

- Foundation
- Ideation
- Creation
- Illustration
- Connection

BUSINESS PRESENTATION REVOLUTION
pSCORE: 5 Stages to Presentation Success

Foundation   Ideation   Creation   Connection

Illustration

Two examples of a structure slide – one boring and uninspiring, and the other visual, clear and attractive

Structure slides are especially important in online presentations when people working from home are likely to be temporarily disturbed; when they put their headset back on, they will quickly want to work out where you are in your flow. A structure slide every few minutes can help them: imagine you are a radio sports commentator who needs to give the score regularly to help listeners who just tuned in.

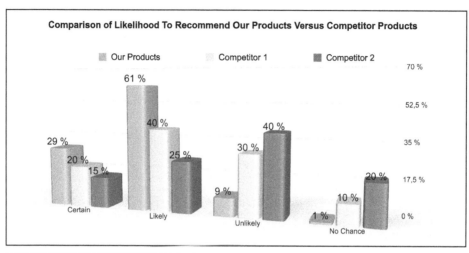

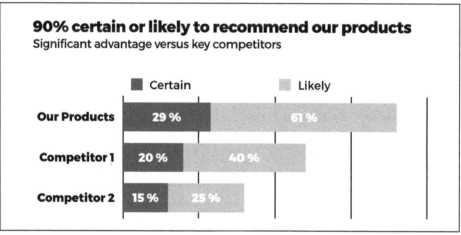

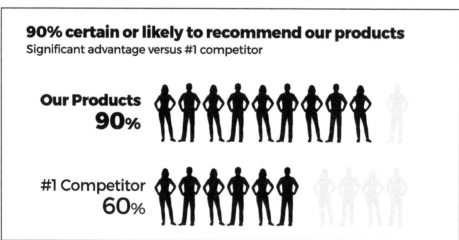

Three ways to show the same data: an ugly graph; a simpler, more attractive chart; and an even simpler visual representation

Data slides

In business, you will need to show numbers in most presentations. Remember that your aim is to communicate the messages behind the numbers, so how you show them is important. If you want to show that employee retention is improving, don't show a five-year attrition rate in a bar chart which, at first glance, seems to indicate bad news because it is going down. Show the retention rate instead, which will immediately look positive. A first look might be all your audience gives your slides – remember that five-second rule.

Note that I call this slide type "data slides" rather than "graph slides." In many cases, you will be able to use Excel-style graphs (ensuring all numbers, labels and colors are clear for your audience), but try to show data more creatively for greater impact.

In the three example slides showing the same data about customer advocacy, the first slide shows an unclear title and an even less clear graph. You could take a long time trying to work out the meaning behind the data. In the second example, our competitive advantage is much clearer, partly through removing unnecessary data points, and partly through better visual design. The third slide shows the data in a more creative and likely more memorable way.

As another example of a creative data slide, with the online wine marketplace Les Grappes (which means "bunches of grapes"), we represented internet wine sales in France, using not bars but different-sized wine glasses, which filled up with wine to reveal the numbers. That was a MAGIQ Moment and a key part of a successful investor pitch.

Diagram slides

You might need to show diagrams – for example, to represent processes. I advise caution with diagrams because they can contain small text and many complicated elements appearing at once.

Where possible, use a "salami approach" for diagrams: have the items build up (using animations, but without movement) slice by slice, so the audience can "get" each part in five seconds and be ready for the next slice. If somebody else is producing your slides, give clear instructions with your sketches so the designer knows which parts to animate and in which order.

Image slides

You might have heard of the Pictorial Superiority Effect, which states that we remember images better than text alone.[25] As long as your images are related to what you are saying, using high-quality photos with powerful imagery can help you communicate a concept memorably. It is even better to add a few words to give the pictures meaning and make your message clear.

For example, Ideas on Stage produced a deck of visual slides for Boston Scientific EMEA President Eric Thépaut, representing the importance of several key behaviors and strengths to their success. One of these slides showed a cheetah leaping, with the caption "Agility." This was so memorable that employees mentioned it regularly throughout the next year. How many C-level presentations have that much impact?

I find that when designing business presentations, there are usually more data slides than image slides; in TED talks, the opposite is often true. Think first whether a data slide or a diagram could work for your presentation; if not, aim for an image slide. Only consider using a text slide if you cannot find anything visual to show your audience.

Two final thoughts on images: first, ensure you have a proper license to use photos, in terms of copyright and image rights. It's best to assume you do not have a license unless you can prove otherwise. Don't just search for images and copy/paste them. Second, never use images that are unrelated to what you are saying. Pretty but irrelevant pictures do not help anyone.[26]

Quotation slides

In many cases, you can make your point using a quotation. In a slide deck I reviewed on the day I am writing this, I found quotations from the company's founder and from clients, as well as from research organizations, consultants and competitors. These all helped to illustrate the key messages. Clients' praise can sell your value better than anything you could say about yourself.

You might also use a quotation from a writer or public figure. This can give credibility to your points and make people think about them in a creative way.

> If your ideas are worth spreading, then presentation matters.
>
> And if you are using visuals to amplify your presentation, then design matters.
>
> **Garr Reynolds**

A quotation slide, with clear text, a photo and no visual pollution

Video slides

If a picture is worth a thousand words, a video is worth a thousand pictures. If you're delivering your presentation online, I usually recommend avoiding video because the refresh rate for your slides often means the video appears jumpy, and the sound may not come through properly. If you want to use video anyway, test it carefully first.

If you are in the same room as your audience, integrating a full-screen video into your slide deck can be impactful. Imagine the following options:

▶ A bullet point saying your services are very good.

▶ A text quotation from a client saying your services are very good.

▶ A client quotation, alongside their photo, saying your services are very good.

▶ A short video of a client saying your services are very good.

Clearly these are in increasing order of effectiveness. A video is also a guaranteed way to "turn over the hourglass" and reset the audience's attention, as long as the video is fairly short.

Text slides

There may be times where your audience doesn't need a graph, or a picture, or a video. There's nothing wrong with text, but treat it like salt: it can enhance what you're saying, but don't add too much. Remember that five-second rule.

I usually use text with images, as quotations or on structure slides. You could also ask a simple question using large, clear text, perhaps in the middle of the slide. While text without images can help the audience understand what you are saying and direct their attention, text slides will quickly be forgotten. Imagine that "agility" slide without the cheetah.

Visual pauses

Lastly, don't forget the World's Best Slide: the pure black slide that focuses your audience's attention back on you and what you are saying. When the audience needs no visual aids, show them none by building visual pauses into your storyboard.

In online presentations, don't share that black slide; instead, plan to stop sharing your slides at those points. It breaks up the flow, resets audience attention, and will allow you to reset it a second time when you start sharing slides again a few minutes later.

Activity: Storyboarding

If you're producing a presentation, it's time to take your script or story-line and create your storyboard.

1. Look back at the outcome of Chapter 4.3, where you identified the parts of your presentation where the audience would benefit from slides as the most appropriate visual aid.

2. Choose a format for your storyboard. You might take your storyline written in a word processor, transform it into a table, and add a storyboard column to the left of your storyline where you can add the slide ideas. The remaining steps in this activity assume you will take this approach; adapt them if you use a different format. You can find a template for this kind of storyboard at **bpr-book.com**.

3. Where you decide not to use slides, fill in the storyboard column with details of any other visual aids you plan to use (e.g., a flipchart, word cloud or survey).

4. Now look at the points where you believe a slide would be helpful to your audience, and consider which of the typical slide types might be most useful: structure slides, data slides, diagram slides, image slides, quotation slides, video slides or text slides.

5. Sketch each slide on paper or a sticky note. When you are happy with each one, take a photo and integrate it into your storyboard.

6. In addition to (or instead of) your sketches, include any necessary instructions as text in the "storyboard" column, so that any designer can understand what you expect them to produce.

7. Review your storyboard to ensure there are enough structure slides, so the audience doesn't feel lost.

8. If possible, leave your storyboard for several hours or a day, then come back to it. You might find you have new ideas or improvement suggestions once your mind has had time to incubate your initial visual thoughts.

You should now have a clear idea of what you want your slides to look like, and either you are ready to prepare these slides in PowerPoint or another slideware application yourself or you have a set of instructions for your designer.

In most companies, you are not entirely free to design these slides as you wish: you are constrained by a corporate slide template, and respecting that standard is as important as turning up to work and answering emails from your boss.

Let's take a quick look at how to handle corporate slide templates while still producing successful slides.

4.6
OVERCOMING CORPORATE TEMPLATES

Uniformly mediocre

Most companies and organizations have their own template for slides, either produced *by* people with little knowledge of good visual communication or – more often – produced *for* people with little knowledge of good visual communication.

Corporate templates are designed to ensure a common "look and feel" across a company's slides and documents. They usually offer several possible layouts, some of which are visual and effective; however, most people look no further than the two default ones: the title slide and the "title + bullets" slide.

Some templates force you to prepare bad slides: they might include too much visual pollution, or a bad color scheme, or a bright white background, or an ugly font. Their main aim is to ensure that all your organization's slides look cohesive. Unfortunately, through a combination of the wrong objectives, poor design and inadequate training, they are usually also ineffective.

What's up with my template?

Your company's slide template may be fantastic, but have you received training on effective use of your template, visual identity and brand guidelines? In most companies I've encountered, people have never learned how to get the best out of their template: either the training is available but nobody knows about it, or it doesn't exist at all.

Your company should have two PowerPoint templates: one with a white background to be used for documents, and another with a dark background to be used for slides for oral presentations. If not, now that you are a Business Presentation Revolutionary perhaps you can take responsibility and argue for change. True leaders are never satisfied with mediocrity.

Think about your organization's slide template (if you have two, consider the one that is designed for oral presentations), and ask yourself the following questions about whether it allows you to produce slides that SCORE with your audience:

▶ Does the slide template use an attractive, distinctive font instead of a boring, tired one?

▶ Is there a 16:9 (widescreen) version of the template?

▶ Does the template avoid unnecessary visual pollution (e.g., slide number, date, name of speaker, logo) on every slide?

▶ Does the template include several possible layouts, including layouts for visual slides?

▶ Is there a set of style guidelines or instructions for using the template?

▶ Does my organization actively train everyone on using the template properly?

If you can answer "yes" to all these questions, then your template is one of the better ones. If not, perhaps one of the following strategies can help you to overcome your template.

Succeeding despite a poor template

If your company's slide template seems to force bad visual design, there are a number of possible strategies open to you, apart from tearing your hair out:

1. **Get the template changed.** If your organization has a poor slide template, take responsibility for improving it. Find whoever is responsible for the template, give them a copy of *Business Presentation Revolution* and either *Slide:ology* or *Presentation Zen Design*, and politely suggest that their current template is fine for documents produced in PowerPoint but that most modern companies also have a different template for presentation slides. By not insulting the current template, you have a better chance of getting them to open their minds to the idea of a different template.

2. **Don't use slides.** If you can't change the template, you could decide to present using a flipchart or a whiteboard, or no visual aids at all. It's not always possible or ideal, but it's better than being stuck with a lot of visual pollution and white light on the wall or screen.

3. **Make the most of your template.** Your template might offer multiple layouts, some of which might be less like "death by PowerPoint" and more like pSCORE. Look for them and see whether they might be a good compromise for you.

4. **Push the boundaries.** Your corporate template exists for a good reason, and it's important to respect that, so accept the choice of font and color palette and keep to them. Use the template faithfully for the title slide and a few others, then see if you can use any of the following tactics to push, but not break, the rules:

   – Insert some pure black slides from time to time as visual pauses (unless your presentation is online). Nobody will insist on a confidentiality notice or slide number on a pure black slide.

- Use the middle of the screen. If you have visual pollution at the top and bottom of your slide that you cannot avoid, you might be able to use the middle part of your slide with more freedom. Make the top and bottom of each slide the same so they fade into the background, and vary the middle part. Before long, the audience will stop noticing the top and bottom.

- "Cheat" selectively. Use your template on some slides, and every now and again show something (like a full-screen image with a few words) without the template elements. You can probably justify not having your corporate logo or page number on a quotation slide with a photo of the author.

Please don't get the impression that I don't like slide templates. I just don't like *most* slide templates. At Ideas on Stage, we design corporate PowerPoint templates, so we understand the value of a good one.

Respecting a coherent visual identity is important. Ideally, you want your slides to be original, but they should also be in harmony with each other, and the elements should be aligned in a visually attractive way: good templates build this in.

Hopefully now you feel capable of succeeding while respecting your corporate template, even if you still aim to get it changed. Now comes the moment you've been waiting for: it's time to transform your storyboard into slides.

4.7
PROFESSIONAL SLIDE DESIGN

Planning for success

This book is not a design guide, nor is it a PowerPoint user manual, so this chapter assumes that, like many senior managers, you are getting someone else to design your slides.

If you're working with a designer, internal or external, you will need to give them clear instructions. I recommend downloading the pSCORE Slide Design Checklist from the *Business Presentation Revolution* website at **bpr-book.com** and completing it together with your storyboard so your designer knows exactly what you expect.

This will ensure your designer knows the software you want them to use, the size of the slides, which template (if any) to use, the color scheme, the preferred fonts, whether using fade transitions or movement are acceptable (I recommend avoiding them in online presentations), and other important details – making their life easier and saving you time later.

Second time lucky

It's an amazing feeling when you get the first version of your slides back from the designer and they look and behave exactly as you expected. It's also a rare feeling.

There may be several reasons why the first version isn't perfect:

1. Your instructions weren't completely clear.

2. Your designer misunderstood or overlooked something.

3. Your designer came up with an innovative design which you don't like or which might need some changes.

4. Your designer's innovative design sparks new ideas for making the deck better.

5. Your designer simply didn't do a good job.

If you're working with a professional slide designer, reason 5 will be rare; more likely, your instructions weren't clear enough or the deck gives you ideas for improvements. Whatever the reasons, the first version is often good but not quite right. This is why you should always give designers enough time to do good work, and to do it twice.

Once you see a version that doesn't fully meet your requirements, and you can explain what needs to change, it's easier for your designer and you to understand exactly what you want and the second version should be good to go.

Don't change your order

There is one final reason for the design not being quite right, and you should guard against this: changing your mind.

When we design slides for clients, we plan to create two versions. I have painful memories of one deck where we ended up with version 17 because the client kept changing his storyline, and therefore his slides. Commissioning your slides and then changing your storyline is like ordering a meal and then asking for something different when it arrives: it creates rework, delays and frustration.

Remember the third key revolution: always produce your story before your slides. Be comfortable with what you are going to say before you begin the storyboarding process.

Final checks

Once you have received a final version of your slides, it is up to you to check everything and run through it to ensure it suits your style and allows you to achieve your objectives.

You should make sure that the fonts work on your computer and on the one that will be used for your live presentation. I have seen fine slides ruined because the presenter missed this step, and the attractive non-standard font – not being installed on the PC used in the amphitheater – was automatically replaced by Arial. Not only did this reduce the attractiveness: it also meant that some words stretched off the screen or over other design elements. Your designer may be able to embed the fonts into your slide deck, but this is not possible with all fonts.

You should check that all transitions and animations (or builds) work as you expect them to, so that you are ready to make the right number of "clicks" to advance them at the right times.

In project management, the initiation phase often takes longer than the execution because it is better to plan properly, allowing you to execute efficiently, than to go ahead with poor planning and then have to change things. Following pSCORE ensures you plan well, making execution fast and smooth, and limiting the need for rework and eleventh-hour changes.

If you have checked your slides and you are happy with them, you are nearly ready to present. Before we move ahead to Connection, let's summarize the Illustration stage.

4.8
ILLUSTRATION: SUMMARY

Now that you have reached the end of the Illustration stage, you should have all the visual aids you need to bring your storyline to life and make it clear and memorable for your audience.

Your slides should SCORE:

▶ **Simple:** Each time you click, your audience should understand all the new content in under five seconds.

▶ **Clear:** Everything is easy to read and understand on a smartphone screen, in terms of size and contrast.

▶ **Original:** Your slides look new and stand out compared to competitors' and other speakers' slides.

▶ **Related:** What you show is related to what you are saying at that time, not before and not after.

▶ **Enjoyable:** Your slides are well-designed and attractive, making your audience enjoy discovering each new slide.

You might also have handouts. No matter how well your slides SCORE, the audience will soon forget what you say and what you show, so it may be wise to give them something to read before your presentation and to leave something behind – but not an ugly slideument that is neither a good slide nor a good document.

Here is a reminder of the pSCORE method for illustrating your storyline:

1. Prepare any necessary handouts for your audience to read before, during or after your presentation.

2. Split your storyline into paragraphs or points, and, for each part, work out whether your audience would benefit from a visual aid to help them understand and/or remember it.

3. Where a visual aid might help, identify the most appropriate kind: a physical action, perhaps with an object; a video; a whiteboard or flipchart; or a slide.

4. Sketch any slides you need on paper or sticky notes.

5. Create a storyboard (perhaps using the template available at **bpr-book.com**) containing your sketches and clear instructions for your designer.

6. Complete the pSCORE Slide Design Checklist available on the book website to ensure you are telling your designer everything they need to know. (If you are designing your own slides, this checklist can still be helpful.)

7. If the first version of your slides is perfect, great! If not, provide clear slide-by-slide instructions showing your designer what to change so the second version is exactly what you need.

8. When you receive the second version, double-check that all transitions, animations and fonts look exactly as they should, and that you are comfortable delivering your presentation with these slides. Fine-tune if necessary.

Now you have your story and slides, it's time to prepare to deliver your presentation to your audience. Like the Foundation stage at the start of the process, the Connection stage is often neglected or rushed, yet it can make the difference between failure and success.

5 CONNECTION

Aim not for **perfect**,
but for **personal.**

5.1
PREPARING TO CONNECT

Are you ready?

If you've carefully followed the advice in the previous chapters, you'll now have a clear, well-structured and memorable talk, tailored to your audience and their burning needs, and illustrated where appropriate with effective visual aids.

You might be tempted to consider yourself ready to get up in front of your audience and deliver it. Perhaps you are. But having the fastest, best designed and most attractive car doesn't guarantee you'll win the race. The performance of the driver is just as important.

 A poor performance can make great material fall flat, but a strong presenter can make average material shine.

What could go wrong?

Assuming that you understand your audience and have prepared a strong presentation that will meet their needs and your objectives within the time allocated, there are three main things that can trip you up:

1. **Failure to prepare**
   Racecar drivers need to prepare for race day with plenty of practice, getting used to their car, and physical and mental training. Presenters should follow the example of Steve Jobs, who spent two days on stage ahead of major keynotes, preparing and rehearsing so he was ready to deliver his best performance.[27]

2. **Over-reliance on technology**
   If a racing crew takes technological risks in the design of the car, the driver might not even finish the race. Similarly, if you rely on a teleprompter, projector or any other technology, there is a chance it will let you down. If you're not prepared to present without technology, you're not prepared to present.

3. **Not being yourself**
   If a racing car doesn't suit the driver's style, or the cockpit is the wrong size for their body, they're likely to have trouble. Likewise, if you try to deliver a presentation that is not compatible with your own style, you are likely to fail.

What does this mean for you?

First, allow yourself time to prepare: while slides are optional, rehearsing is necessary. Second, make sure you are ready to speak even if your slides fail. And third, work out your own presenting style and improve within that style, rather than trying to be somebody you're not. We'll take a look at presenter styles in the next chapter.

 Success on stage is often as simple as being yourself and taking the time to rehearse until you are comfortable with your talk.

What could go right?

Before we look at how to prepare, let's take a moment to focus on what could go right.

This is a question of mindset. Too often, speakers approach their presentation worried about what might go wrong: forgetting their speech, getting a tough question, overrunning, etc.

Think instead of the opportunities. What could happen if everything goes well? Perhaps your audience will applaud at the end or congratulate you afterwards. Perhaps you will gain funding for your project or your client will want to work with your company. Perhaps you'll be invited to present again or even be promoted.

A presentation is a fabulous chance to make a name for yourself. As Harvey Coleman pointed out, business career success requires performance, image and exposure – and presentations are a powerful way to improve your image and gain more exposure, the two most important success factors.[28]

 Focusing on what could go right, and visualizing that success, will make you feel more comfortable about your presentation, calm your nerves, and prepare you to deliver more powerfully and confidently.

The importance of connection

Too many businesspeople treat presentations as performances, like an actor playing Hamlet.

No business audience enjoys a monologue or a speaker who appears to be talking to themselves. Remember: it's not your presentation – it's theirs. Since communication is more about what they receive than what you send, it's vital to build a connection with them so they are part of your presentation and paying full attention.

This means you need to pay attention to your audience and how they are reacting to your messages – and adapt your presentation accordingly. Aim to interact with your audience as much as possible and to bring them into the presentation. The more you can connect on a personal, human level with your audience, the more likely they will be to overlook your imperfections and want you to succeed – and the more attentively they will listen.

Remember your transformational objectives. What do you need your audience to do, feel and believe? Your objective is not to deliver your presentation exactly as planned: it is to transform your audience.

 Prepare your presentation thoroughly, and rehearse it several times. Once you know it well, you will feel able to be fully present with your audience and react and adapt as necessary to achieve your objectives. Successful improvisation depends on preparation.

Let go of perfection

There is no such thing as a perfect presentation. Just prepare and rehearse it enough to know it well and ensure your messages come from the heart, not the head. If you can focus on delivering not just the syllables of your words but also the meaning behind them, then you are ready. Do not overdo it, though. Your audience does not expect perfection, and if you can create a strong connection with them they will see you as more human. Focus not on trying to speak perfectly but on making a personal connection with your audience, one member at a time.

With the importance of connection in mind, the next chapter will cover how to make your presentation delivery SCORE with your audience, and breathe life and energy into your story: the "telling" part of storytelling.

5.2
HOW TO SCORE ON STAGE

In the Creation and Illustration stages, we focused on the five pSCORE success factors, and they are equally relevant in the Connection stage. Just like your story and your slides, your delivery must reach the same five goals: Simple. Clear. Original. Related. Enjoyable.

Whether your presentation will take place on stage or online, let's take a look at what speaking success looks and sounds like.

Simple

When it comes to speaking, simplicity means using straightforward language that your audience can easily understand, speaking in short sentences, and not using more words than you need.

This is more important than ever before: today, you will often be presenting to people from different countries, perhaps not in your first language, or perhaps not in theirs. Where once it was considered a sign of intelligence to use complicated vocabulary and rhetoric to impress your audience, today it is more important to use plain language so they can understand you.

Avoid jargon, acronyms and expressions that may not be clear to everyone, like "leftfield" or "back to square one." Remember that in an oral presentation, long sentences are hard to follow, especially for people who are not fluent in the language. Use short, simple sentences, followed by pauses so the audience can digest what you said, what you mean and – most importantly – what it means to them.

Lastly, simplicity means not using a hundred words when ten will do.

If you keep your language simple, with short sentences and pauses, you'll give your audience the best chance of understanding your key messages and their importance.

Clear

If the words you choose are simple to understand, you are on the right track. You also need to say them clearly, speaking loudly and slowly enough so your audience can easily decipher each syllable.

Always remember that you are speaking to the person furthest from you – not to the front row. If you are speaking online, you should use a quality microphone and check the levels to make sure you are easy to hear.

Even if the audience can hear everything you say, they might not understand you if you speak like a high-speed train. Allow your audience time – not only to hear each syllable but to understand each sentence and digest each point. Speaking more slowly has the added benefit of making you appear more convincing, as long as you don't overdo it. Teenagers often speak in a sprint; leaders give every word the importance it deserves.

Clarity also means leaving pauses, especially at the end of sentences. Pauses are the most important parts of your presentation, helping you and your audience to breathe, and helping them to understand, digest and file away your key messages. Pauses accentuate what you say between them.

If everyone in your audience can clearly hear and understand every syllable, your messages have a chance of hitting their target.

Original

To become an even better version of yourself when speaking in public, you must first understand and accept your own natural style and work to improve within it.

Are you more comfortable giving a serious talk or trying to entertain your audience? Both of these styles are perfectly fine in business, although not always in the same contexts. Don't try to entertain people if that's not your style or if you're worried people won't laugh or smile. There's nothing wrong with being serious, as long as you are convincing rather than boring.

Are you more comfortable learning your speech or improvising most of it? The first TED talk we worked on at Ideas on Stage (we're now way past the 500 mark) was for a well-known TV presenter. We quickly realized that he was not a learner. Give him a stage and a microphone, and he'll improvise brilliantly, but give him a script and ask him to stick to it, and he will find it challenging.

We've also seen many speakers who are more comfortable knowing their speech word for word and who freeze if asked to improvise. Most of us are somewhere between these two extremes.

Wherever you are on this scale between learners and improvisers, there is no "ideal" style. The only wrong style is one which is wrong for you, and it's up to you to find which style is right for you.

Nobody is better at being you than you. Find your style, accept it, hone it, and don't attempt to be someone you're not. The audience doesn't want an imitation of someone else – they want the authentic you. Only then can you truly make a connection.

Related

While your storyline and messages should already be tailored to your audience's needs and context, the way you act and speak can help you to make a stronger connection with them.

There are two reliable ways to relate to your audience while presenting. Firstly, your delivery should match the context of the presentation as much as it matches your own personal style. While following your own style, you will naturally adopt a different tone in different situations. You might want to be upbeat and energetic if you aim to motivate your employees, but you should sound less enthusiastic if you are announcing layoffs. Similarly, dress appropriately for the context, and you will make a better impression and a stronger connection.

The second way to relate to your audience is to interact with them as often as possible, especially in online meetings where it is easier for them to "switch off." Make them a part of the communication: passive listeners rarely listen attentively.

For in-person presentations, aim to make regular eye contact with each audience member (or – for a large audience – with someone in each zone of your room). Look each person in the eyes for a sentence, and then move on to someone in another part of the room for the next sentence. In online meetings, though, remember to look at your camera more than at your screen: when you look directly into your camera, the audience will think you are looking at them.

You can also make a connection with gestures. While speaking, your default position should be what I call the "catcher position," like a catcher in cricket: your elbows bent at 90°, your hands apart and your palms facing upwards, as if ready to catch a ball. From the catcher position, you can make various hand gestures and then return to this position. It is also an open position, which creates an invisible connection with the audience.

In online meetings, hand gestures can be harder to use because the audience might only see your head and shoulders. You should therefore be especially expressive with your facial gestures, smiling whenever appropriate.

 When you make and maintain a connection, the audience will be part of the communication instead of passive observers, and they will perceive what you say as something related to them.

Enjoyable

If the audience doesn't enjoy listening to you, they won't listen. Nobody pays full attention to someone boring – no matter how good their story and slides are.

 Time is money, but attention is the true currency of leaders.

What makes a speaker enjoyable to watch and listen to? Three simple elements: comfort, passion and variation.

Comfort

The first element is how comfortable the speaker appears to be. If the speaker is moving from side to side with no stability, doesn't know what to do with their hands, has trouble finding their words, ums and ahs, and never smiles, then they will appear poorly prepared and unimpressive. Audiences will feel disrespected by the lack of preparation, and nobody listens to speakers who make a bad impression.

On the other hand, we feel positive about a speaker who is stable, makes strong and clear gestures, knows their talk well enough to sound natural and smiles at appropriate times. The audience is more likely to listen to this kind of speaker.

Passion

A speaker who expresses no passion receives no attention. If you don't appear to care about your subject or your audience, or believe in what you are saying, the audience will not care or believe any more than you do. You cannot be convincing unless you look and sound convinced yourself.

We transmit our emotions to our audience.[29] When a speaker appears bored and passionless, the audience will feel the same way. Likewise, if you appear enthusiastic, motivated, passionate and happy to be there, the audience will likely feel just as positive.

Your communication should come from the heart, not the head. Focus not just on the syllables of your words but on their meaning, and deliver the emotion behind the words to connect with your audience, engage them and transform them. Reveal your human side and show that you care about what you are saying. If there is one thing more contagious than boredom, it's passion.

Variation

If monotony generates boredom, variation generates attention. Listening to a monotonous speech is like driving through a flat desert; listening to a speech full of variation is like driving through a beautiful national park with a new vista at every curve. We pay attention when things change and when each sentence delivers something different.

You might already have chosen to vary your storyline and slides, breaking up the flow and turning over the hourglass of the audience's attention on a regular basis so your presentation is not just a monologue with slides. You can also vary the way you speak and move. If monotony means always speaking in the same tone and at the same speed, a good speaker will vary both.

▶ **Tone:** Aim to make each sentence like a melody, not a single repeated note. In most languages, you will find the tone should rise before a comma and fall at the end of each sentence. It is more interesting to listen to a speaker who varies their tone than one who speaks like a 1980s computer.

▶ **Speed:** Even while varying your tone, if you maintain a constant rhythm and speed you will sound monotonous. Vary your speed within and between sentences, using pauses wisely, so the audience hears more of a piano concerto than a regular drumbeat.

Now that you know what speaking success looks like, and how important it is to make a connection with your audience, let's finish with some practical advice on preparing to deliver your presentation.

5.3
MAKING THE CONNECTION

The big day approaches

Before you take the stage, you need to be comfortable. Audiences don't appreciate speakers who haven't prepared properly, don't know their presentation well enough, and are visibly worrying about what to say next.

There are several simple actions you can take before your presentation to maximize your own comfort and help you to deliver a better talk. We can remember these as the 3 S's: Serenity, Space and Support.

Serenity

Whether you prefer to improvise or learn your speech, you should rehearse it aloud several times, filming yourself if you can, and making sure you take no more than 90% of the time allocated for your presentation (not including any time for questions and answers). The fifth run-through will be much better than the first, and you will be more comfortable with the flow of your presentation and better equipped to react, adapt and improvise if needed.

If preparing your presentation is like mixing the ingredients for a cake, then rehearsing is like baking it. Most cakes are not edible raw, but you should not burn them either. Rehearse enough, but closer to five times than fifty. You're aiming for a personal connection, not a perfect delivery.

In particular, rehearse your introduction and conclusion, even if you aim to improvise much of your presentation. The beginning is where you will feel the most stress, and where the audience will form an initial impression of you, so knowing your introduction will give you the best chance of a strong first impression. Equally, knowing your conclusion well should make their final impression just as positive.

You should also prepare a cue-card: write a few words to remind you of the flow of your presentation on a small piece of paper to keep in your pocket. This way, you won't worry about forgetting what to say – and because you will feel more comfortable, you'll remember your flow more easily. If you don't write a cue-card, you might regret it.

Space

Familiarizing yourself with the place or online platform in which you will be presenting will help you feel more relaxed. Try to get access to the room, stage or application in advance so you are not discovering it at the start of your presentation.

Support

The people handling the technology are your friends, as long as you seek them out in advance, ask them about any limitations and make sure they know what you need from them. For a presentation with a live audience, this means the microphones, lighting, sound and screen. For an online presentation, it means the people who will be responsible for the online platform, screen sharing, spotlighting your video and making sure only the right microphones are live.

Once these important people are properly briefed and on your side, you will feel ready and calm. Knowing that they have tested your slides in real conditions will give you one less thing to worry about. (Hat tip to my Ideas on Stage colleague Michael Rickwood who coined the 3 S's.)

The big day arrives

On the day of your presentation, if you've prepared properly, you should feel ready. It's too late to change everything, so you need to feel confident that you've followed a strong process, that you aimed your presentation at this audience and their needs, and that you've designed it expressly to achieve your transformational objectives.

Keep these objectives in mind. Remember: what do you want them to believe, feel and do differently after your presentation? Success is not getting to your last slide in the time available and saying all the words you planned to say: success is achieving your transformational objectives, no matter how you do it.

This may mean that you need to adapt after you've started your presentation. If you've prepared well, you will be able to react to your audience's questions and their own reactions. In some cases, you might find they need more detail or an extra example to understand your messages. As long as you have left yourself a little time, you can and should do this. It is better to go off-script and achieve your objectives than to stick to what you'd planned but fail.

Here are some final tips to help you to succeed on your big day:

▶ **Arrive early.** Leaving plenty of time will reduce your stress and allow you time to run through your cue-card a few times before you are called on stage (or asked to present in the meeting room).

▶ **Try to greet members of the audience before you start.** It's remarkable how much it can help to know several people in the audience are on your side.

▶ **Don't drink coffee before presenting.** Caffeine increases your stress, makes you ramble, and dries your throat and mouth, reducing the resonance of your voice.[30, 31] Also avoid carbonated drinks, especially if you have a microphone. Instead, drink plenty of still water.

▶ **Prepare yourself physically.** If possible, take a brisk walk before you go on stage so your body and mind are in action mode. If you are presenting virtually, set up your camera so you can deliver your presentation standing up: this will give you more energy and allow you to transmit that energy to your audience.

▶ **Manage your time.** If you don't have a countdown timer on stage or a clock on your PowerPoint presenter view, make sure you have a clock clearly visible so you know how long you have left while you're presenting. Aim to finish a little early: your audience will be as grateful as they would be annoyed if you ran over time.

 Above all, enjoy your presentation. If you enjoy it, so will they.

After the presentation

You've delivered your talk, and survived, and you've done your best to achieve your transformational objectives. Congratulations! But your work is not yet complete.

A few post-presentation actions can help you cement those transformations and learn from the experience so you can deliver an even more effective presentation next time.

▶ **Deliver your handouts.** Sending a standalone document a day or three after your presentation will remind the audience of what you said and why, and it gives you another opportunity to explain your call to action.

▶ **Ask for feedback.** You might not want to ask your whole audience to rate your presentation, but a few members of the audience might be able and willing to offer constructive, honest comments. They are unlikely to offer unsolicited feedback, so make a point of asking for their suggestions.

▶ **Think what you could have done differently.** Did you end up with unnecessary slides or try to say too much? Did your introduction hit hard enough? Did you spend enough time rehearsing? Be honest about what you could have done better, and remember these points when you begin preparing your next presentation.

Your presentation wasn't perfect. No presentation is. Although you should treat every presentation as an opportunity to improve, do not waste energy seeking perfection or worrying about your performance. Simply seek to make a personal connection with people, and show that you care about them and what you are asking them to do, and you will be well on the road to success.

5.4
CONNECTION: SUMMARY

It's easier to describe what successful speakers do than to do it yourself, but learning to speak professionally is like learning to drive a car: you need to be aware of what's happening around you, know where you are heading, keep going despite distractions, take detours where necessary, and keep control of your hands and feet even though they have different things to do at the same time. It's not easy. It takes plenty of practice, and you can't learn to drive a car or to speak in public only from a book. You have to do it.

That's why this section is shorter than the previous ones. To supplement it, you'll find video resources to help you to understand how to speak more clearly, comfortably and convincingly at **bpr-book.com**, and I encourage you to watch them.

Here is a brief summary of the key points of this all-important final stage:

1. Good speakers SCORE when speaking:

   – **Simple:** use short sentences and plain language, with regular pauses, and no ums or ahs

   – **Clear:** make sure they can hear and understand every syllable

   – **Original:** find your own style, accept it and hone it

- **Related:** create a connection through interaction, eye contact and gestures, while dressing appropriately

- **Enjoyable:** prepare well so you appear comfortable; show your passion and vary your tone and rhythm

2. As the big day approaches, focus on the 3 S's:

- **Serenity:** rehearse your presentation several times focusing especially on the introduction and conclusion, and prepare a short handwritten cue-card

- **Space:** get to know the room, stage or platform where you will be presenting

- **Support:** connect with the technical people and brief them, so they know what you need and can help you succeed

3. On the big day, arrive early, try to greet some audience members before you begin, avoid coffee, prepare yourself physically, and manage your time well.

4. After the presentation, deliver your handouts, ask for feedback, and note what you could do differently next time.

Above all, treat every presentation you give as an opportunity to practice and improve. Nobody was born a great presenter. If you're amazed at how professional speakers appear at TED or WikiStage or some major online product launches, and feel you aren't yet at the same level, just remember that those presenters had to work hard to become that good, and they usually have presentation specialists to help them.

 I have never yet met anyone who did not have the potential to become a strong speaker. With time, effort and perhaps some speaker coaching, you can become the kind of presenter people look forward to listening to.

CONCLUSION AND NEXT STEPS

The rest is up to you

Congratulations on making it to the end of this book. By now, you should have developed an intolerance for poor presentations, an understanding of what success looks like, and a desire to rise above the average, boring and unsuccessful.

It is important to remember, however, that you are still just beginning your journey as a Business Presentation Revolutionary. This book is an introduction to the new arts of presenting, an overview of the Presentation SCORE Method, and an encouragement to go further, but it is not the whole story.

There's always more to learn about business storytelling, slide design and speaking, not to mention education and online meetings. For you, as an aspiring leader, this is not a soft skill: it is a key part of your role, and the fastest road to success. How far you travel along that road depends on how much time and effort you are prepared to invest.

It's up to you to continue the story. This book is only a guide to help you find your own way to a better presentation destination.

You are not alone

Communication may be one of your most important responsibilities, but it is not your full-time specialty. Just as those who climb Everest partner with local climbers to help them reach the summit, you might reach greater heights, faster, if you do not make your presentation journey alone.

Most leaders don't have the time or focus to produce a compelling storyline, or sketch a storyboard, let alone design attractive and effective slides. World-class athletes have coaches, nutritionists, physiotherapists and other professionals helping them, not because of weakness, but to build their strengths. Working with a presentation coach or a designer is a sign that you understand communication is a key part of your role as a leader, and you want to turn it into a strength.

Lastly, it's hard to create a revolution alone: you will make more impact (and sit through fewer boring presentations) if you convince your colleagues to join you in this new way of presenting. You might recruit new Business Presentation Revolutionaries simply by presenting brilliantly and inspiring your audiences to follow your example. You might also raise awareness by sharing the articles and videos on the book's website.

What? So what? What next?

Finally, I should "drink my own champagne" and give you a conclusion, just as I would if I were presenting, using "What? So what? What next?" and finishing with an inspirational last line and of course the magic words: "Thank you."

What?

Most presentations fail, yet communication is one of a leader's most important responsibilities, so we should all learn to present effectively.

Apply these five major revolutions to make your presentations stand out for the right reasons:

 It's not your presentation – it's theirs.

 Aim not to inform, but to transform.

 Create your storyline before your slides.

 Don't confuse slides and documents.

 Aim not for perfect but for personal.

The Presentation SCORE Method, or pSCORE, is a proven process for creating and delivering inspirational presentations, and leaders have used it successfully across different industries and functions, online, on stage and in the boardroom. If you follow this simple five-stage method, from Foundation through Ideation, Creation, Illustration and Connection, your presentations will be Simple, Clear, Original, Related and Enjoyable, and your audiences will be transformed.

So what?

As a leader, a manager or a salesperson, your success depends on the actions of others. The low level of most presentations offers an opportunity to those who learn how to get people's attention, communicate strongly and transform their audiences. If you can learn to change what people believe, feel and do, there is no limit to what you can achieve.

What next?

Follow pSCORE to prepare your next presentation, and use every talk as an opportunity to practice, experiment and learn.

Seek expert help from a presentation specialist, if necessary, to help you apply pSCORE in your company.

Read and watch the additional materials available at **bpr-book.com**.

Finally, think about friends and colleagues who might also benefit from joining the Business Presentation Revolution.

You are at the beginning of your journey to becoming the best presenter you can be. Following this path is a small investment that will make a big difference for your career. I urge you to keep going. You won't regret it. And your audiences will thank you.

REFERENCES

1. Items 1-4 in the list reference J Medina, *Brain Rules* (Pear Press, 2009), 84-89.
2. Item 5 in the list references J Medina, *Brain Rules* (Pear Press, 2009), 130.
3. Item 6 in the list references J Schwabish, *Better Presentations* (Columbia University Press, 2017), 24.
4. J Bigelow and A Poremba, "Achilles' Ear? Inferior Human Short-Term and Recognition Memory in the Auditory Modality," PLoS ONE, 9 (2), e89914, https://journals.plos.org/plosone/article?id=10.1371/journal.pone.0089914, accessed 19 May 2021.
5. J Bariso, "Jeff Bezos Knows How to Run a Meeting. Here's How He Does It," Inc. (30 April 2018), www.inc.com/justin-bariso/jeff-bezos-knows-how-to-run-a-meeting-here-are-his-three-simple-rules.html, accessed April 2021.
6. G Wallas, *The Art of Thought* (Solis Press, 2014).
7. P Waknell, "The Three Magic Ingredients of Amazing Presentations" (November 2019), www.ted.com/talks/phil_waknell_the_3_magic_ingredients_of_amazing_presentations, accessed 22 May 2021.
8. DH Pink, *A Whole New Mind* (Marshall Cavendish International, 2008), 101-104.
9. G Reynolds, "Lessons from the bamboo," TEDxTokyo (2011), www.tedxtokyo.com/tedxtokyo_talk/lessons-from-the-bamboo, accessed 22 May 2021.
10. B Gates, "Mosquitos, malaria and education" (February 2009), www.ted.com/talks/bill_gates_mosquitos_malaria_and_education, accessed 22 May 2021.
11. G Reynolds, *Presentation Zen*, 3rd edition (New Riders, 2020), 66-68.

12. G Reynolds, "Why Storytelling Matters," TEDxKyoto (30 October 2014), www.youtube.com/watch?v=YbV3b-l1sZs, accessed 22 May 2021.

13. S Batra, "Can we conquer tuberculosis?," TEDxWBG (20 October 2014), www.youtube.com/watch?v=3c_56Ka-Npw, accessed 22 May 2021.

14. J Oliver, "Teach every child about food" (February 2010), www.ted.com/talks/jamie_oliver_teach_every_child_about_food, accessed 22 May 2021.

15. R Price and M Meisenzahl, "The first iPhone was announced 13 years ago today – here's how Steve Jobs introduced it," Insider (9 January 2020), www.insider.com/watch-steve-jobs-first-iphone-10-years-ago-legendary-keynote-macworld-sale-2017-6, accessed 21 May 2021.

16. A Marchac, "Beyond Esthetics," TEDxESCP (30 May 2012), www.youtube.com/watch?v=R4qVSlFkZgg, accessed May 22 2021.

17. P Waknell, "What are the secrets of a great WikiTalk?" (March 2013), www.wikistage.org/video/what-are-the-secrets-of-a-great-wikitalk, accessed 22 May 2021.

18. G Reynolds, *Presentation Zen*, 3rd edition (New Riders, 2020), 72-74.

19. J Medina, *Brain Rules* (Pear Press, 2009), 84-89.

20. N Duarte, *Slidedocs* (Duarte, 2014), https://duarte.com/slidedocs, accessed 22 May 2021.

21. Sir K Robinson, "Do schools kill creativity?" (February 2006), www.ted.com/talks/sir_ken_robinson_do_schools_kill_creativity, accessed 22 May 2021.

22. N Duarte, *Slide:ology* (O'Reilly Media, 2008); G Reynolds, *Presentation Zen Design*, 2nd edition (New Riders, 2014).

23. J Schwabish, *Better Data Visualizations* (Columbia University Press, 2021).

24. J Schwabish, *Better Presentations* (Columbia University Press, 2017), 135-143.

25. J Medina, *Brain Rules* (Pear Press, 2009), 233-235.

26. J Schwabish, *Better Presentations* (Columbia University Press, 2017), 24.

27. C Gallo, *The Presentation Secrets of Steve Jobs*, hardcover edition (McGraw-Hill 2010), 180.

28. H Coleman, *Empowering Yourself,* 2nd edition (AuthorHouse, 2010), 21-24.

29. E Prochazkova and ME Kret, "Connecting minds and sharing emotions through mimicry: A neurocognitive model of emotional contagion," *Neuroscience & Biobehavioral Reviews,* 80 (September 2017), 99-114, www.sciencedirect.com/science/article/pii/S0149763416306704, accessed 22 May 2021.

30. W Lovallo et al, "Cortisol responses to mental stress, exercise, and meals following caffeine intake in men and women," *Pharmacology Biochemistry and Behavior,* 83/3 (March 2006), 441-447, https://doi.org/10.1016/j.pbb.2006.03.005, accessed 22 May 2021.

31. E Hartney, "Side Effects of Caffeine," Verywell Mind (4 March 2021), www.verywellmind.com/what-are-the-side-effects-of-caffeine-21847, accessed 22 May 2021.

ACKNOWLEDGEMENTS

I am indebted to many people who have helped develop me to a point where I have something I feel is worth sharing, assisted (and prodded) me to write this book, and supported me over a long and often interrupted writing process.

I must begin with those giants on whose shoulders I stand, and while I cannot cite all the presentation specialists, past and present, who have influenced me, I must single out Nancy Duarte, who blazed a trail for presentation experts many years before we founded Ideas on Stage, and Garr Reynolds, whose masterpiece *Presentation Zen* inspired us to action and who has been a great support since I first met him in 2010.

My colleagues at Ideas on Stage have been instrumental in testing and honing our techniques with many more clients than I alone could work with, in giving invaluable feedback on the various drafts of this book, and in keeping our clients happy while I concentrated on the writing process. In alphabetical order, therefore, a million thanks to Marine Bénard, Rose Bloomfield, Ricardo Bonis Calvo, Marion Chapsal, Pierre Morsa, Andrea Pacini, Vanessa Querville, Michael Rickwood, Joe Ross, Edoardo Sala, Camille Spokojny and Frédéric-Pascal Stein.

My thanks also to several clients and friends who have given invaluable input, ideas, advice and support: Nicolas Beau, Johannes Bittel, Isaac Getz, Richard Lancaster, Patricia Lane, Alex Linley, Celin Roisin Reilly, Jackie Saunders, Philippe Trolez and too many others to mention.

My final and most heartfelt thanks must go to my wonderful parents, who gave me such a strong foundation in life, to my sons for putting up with me and my jokes, and especially to my dear late wife Nadège, for her love and her unflinching support over the years, both to follow my dream with Ideas on Stage and to share my ideas in this book, which I humbly dedicate to her.

THE AUTHOR

Phil Waknell is Chief Inspiration Officer at Ideas on Stage, the leading presentation specialists, working with many of the world's top companies, speakers and start-ups, as well as helping hundreds of presenters at all types of conferences, from TED to corporate events.

Phil co-founded Ideas on Stage in 2010 with business consultant and ace designer Pierre Morsa. It quickly became a world-renowned presentation design, coaching and training company, based on a mix of business storytelling, high-impact slide design and powerful speaking coaching, with a dash of real business experience, a large dose of creativity and a dedication to delighting clients.

Before Ideas on Stage, Phil spent several years as an IT manager with Procter & Gamble and six years with Hewlett-Packard in international account and sales leadership roles. He has lived and worked in the United Kingdom, France, Belgium, Bulgaria and Japan. He holds an Executive MBA from HEC Paris and a languages degree from the University of Leeds. Despite living outside his native UK since the last century and becoming French enough to understand the rules of belote, he still loves cricket, curry, and beer without bubbles.

While based in Europe, Phil teaches, trains and speaks all over the world about the art of presenting, in English and French. In addition to giving

Ideas on Stage courses and keynotes, and helping business leaders and start-ups with their most important presentations and pitches, he teaches business communication at HEC Paris Executive Education and EMLyon Executive Education.

Contact Ideas on Stage if you'd like help revolutionizing presentations where you work. From their offices in the US and across Europe, Phil and his colleagues work with clients all over the world in several languages. You can find them at:

⊕ **www.ideasonstage.com**

▣ **www.linkedin.com/in/waknell**

▢ **@philwaknell**

▢ **@ideasonstage**

IDEAS ON STAGE

PARIS ▸ LONDON ▸ LA ▸ BARCELONA ▸ MILAN

Some training courses are based on books. This book is based on a training course.

Phil and his colleagues at Ideas on Stage have given our flagship *Business Presentation Revolution* course to companies, start-ups, associations, business schools and social entrepreneurs for many years.

We coach and train in English, French, Spanish and Italian, online or in person.

If you'd like to boost your organization with a proven hands-on training course that brings pSCORE to life, inspire your people with a powerful keynote talk or webinar, or wow people with your own presentations, we'd love to hear from you.

Contact us via our our web site mentioning the hashtag *#businesspresentationrevolutionary* for a 5% discount on our courses and keynotes.

www.ideasonstage.com